ISRAEL'S
SACRED
TERRORISM

About the Author

Livia Rokach, an Italian writer and journalist of Palestinian origin, is the author of *No to a Golden Ghetto, Vietnam: Against Genocide, The Open Wounds* and *The Proofs.* Prior to her death in April 1984, Ms. Rokach was a fellow of the Amsterdam-based Transnational Insititute, an affiliate of the Institute for Policy Studies in Washington, DC, and a contributor to several international publications, including *Al-Fajar.*

AAUG Information Paper Series: No. 23

Livia Rokach

ISRAEL'S
SACRED
TERRORISM

Third Edition

A study based on
Moshe Sharett's *Personal Diary*
and other documents

With a Foreword by
Noam Chomsky

 PRESS

ASSOCIATION OF ARAB-AMERICAN UNIVERSITY GRADUATES, INC.
Belmont, Massachusetts

First published in the United States of America by 🕮 Press

Library of Congress Cataloging in Publication Data

Rokach, Livia.
    Israel's sacred terrorism.

    (AAUG information paper series; no. 23)

    1. Jewish-Arab relations—1949–1967. 2. Sharett, Moshe, 1894–1965. I. Sharett, Moshe, 1894–1965. Yoman ishi. English. Selections. 1986. II. Title. III. Series.
DS119.7.R64 1986   327.569404917'4924   85-19946
ISBN 0-937694-70-3

Design and typesetting by Accugraphics   102409

To all the Palestinian victims of Israel's unholy terrorism, whose sacrifice, suffering and ongoing struggle will yet prove to be the pangs of the rebirth of Palestine.

CONTENTS

FOREWORD

History, particularly recent history, is characteristically presented to the general public within the framework of a doctrinal system based on certain fundamental dogmas. In the case of the totalitarian societies, the point is too obvious to require comment. The situation is more intriguing in societies that lack cruder forms of repression and ideological control. The United States, for example, is surely one of the least repressive societies of past or present history with respect to freedom of inquiry and expression. Yet only rarely will an analysis of crucial historical events reach a wide audience unless it conforms to certain doctrines of the faith.

"The United States always starts out with good intentions." With this ritual incantation, a liberal critic of American interventionism enters the area of permissible debate, of thinkable thoughts (in this case, William Pfaff, "Penalty of Interventionism," *International Herald Tribune,* February 1979). To accept the dogma, a person who is unable to tolerate more than a limited degree of internal contradiction must studiously avoid the documentary record, which is ample in a free society—for example, the record of high-level planning exhibited in the Pentagon Papers, particularly the record of the early years of U.S. involvement in the 1940s and early 1950s when the basic outlines of strategy were developed and formulated. Within the scholarly professions and the media the intelligentsia can generally be counted on to close ranks; they will refuse to submit to critical analysis the doctrines of the faith, prune the historical and documentary record so as to insulate these doctrines from examination, and proceed to present a version of history that is safely free from institutional critique or analysis. Occasional departures from orthodoxy are of little moment as long as they are confined to narrow circles that can be ignored, or dismissed as "irresponsible" or "naive" or "failing to comprehend the complexities of history," or otherwise identified with familiar code-words as beyond the pale.

Though relations between Israel and the United States have not been devoid of conflict, still there is no doubt that there has been, as is often said, a "special relationship." This is obvious at the material level, as measured by flow of capital and armaments, or as measured by diplomatic support, or by joint operations, as when Israel acted to defend crucial U.S. interests in the Middle East at the time of the 1970 crisis involving Jordan, Syria and the Palestinians. The special relationship appears at the ideological level as well. Again with rare exceptions, one must adopt certain doctrines of the faith to enter the arena of debate, at least before any substantial segment of the public.

The basic doctrine is that Israel has been a hapless victim—of terrorism, of military attack, of implacable and irrational hatred. It is not uncommon for well-informed American political analysts to write that Israel has been attacked four times by its neighbors, including even 1956. Israel is sometimes chided for its response to terrorist attack, a reaction that is deemed wrong though understandable. The belief that Israel may have had a substantial role in initiating and perpetuating violence and conflict is expressed only far from the mainstream, as a general rule. In discussing the backgrounds of the 1956 war, Nadav Safran of Harvard University, in a work that is fairer than most, explains that Nasser "seemed bent on mobilizing Egypt's military resources and leading the Arab countries in an assault on Israel." The Israeli raid in Gaza in February 1955 was "retaliation" for the hanging of Israeli saboteurs in Egypt—it was only six years later, Safran claims, that it became known that they were indeed Israeli agents. The immediate background for the conflict is described in terms of fedayeen terror raids and Israeli retaliation. The terror organized by Egyptian intelligence "contributed significantly to Israel's decision to go to war in 1956 and was the principal reason for its refusal to evacuate the Gaza Strip" (*Israel—The Embattled Ally*, Cambridge: Harvard University Press, 1978).

To maintain such doctrines as these, or the analysis of alleged fact that conform to them, it is necessary scrupulously to avoid crucial documentation. Safran, in his 600-page study, makes no use of major sources such as the diaries that Livia Rokach reviews here, relevant parts of which had been made public in 1974, or the captured Egyptian documents published in Israel in 1975, or other sources that undermine these analyses (see footnotes 19, 20). Much the same is true of the mainstream scholarly literature and journalism fairly generally.

Moshe Sharett's diary, to which Livia Rokach's monograph is devoted, is undoubtedly a major documentary source. It remains outside of "official history"—that version of history that reaches more than a tiny audience of people unsatisfied by conventional doctrine. It is only reasonable to predict that this will remain true in the United States as long as the "special relationship" persists. If, on the other hand, Israel had been, say, an ally of the Soviet Union, then Sharett's revelations would quickly become common knowledge, just as no one would speak of the Egyptian attack on Israel in 1956.

In studying the process of policy formation in any state, it is common to find a rough division between relatively hard-line positions that urge the use of force and violence to attain state ends, and "softer" approaches that advocate diplomatic or commercial methods to attain the same objectives—a distinction between "the Prussians" and "the traders," to borrow terms that Michael Klare has suggested in his work on U.S. foreign policy. The goals are basically the same; the measures advocated differ, at least to a degree, a fact that may ultimately bear on the nature of the ends pursued. Sharett was an advocate of the "soft" approach. His defeat in internal Israeli politics reflected the ascendancy of the positions of Ben Gurion, Dayan and others who were not reluctant to use force to attain their goals. His diaries give a very revealing picture of the developing conflict, as he perceived it, and offer an illuminating insight into the early history of the state of Israel, with ramifications that reach to the present, and beyond. Livia Rokach has performed a valuable service in making this material readily available, for the first time, to those who are interested in discovering the real world that lies behind "official history."

NOAM CHOMSKY
January 1, 1980

PREFACE TO THIS EDITION _____

In pursuit of its objectives of disseminating accurate information about the Middle East, the Association of Arab-American University Graduates, Inc. thought it in the public interest to publish this study, which analyzes Israeli-Arab relations in the late 1940s and 1950s in the light of the personal diary of Moshe Sharett.[1] Head of the Jewish Agency's Political Department from 1933 to 1948, Sharett became Israel's first foreign minister (1948–1956), under David Ben Gurion), and was prime minister in 1954 and 1955.

Since this book was first published five years ago, a number of occurrences have taken place that point up its enduring significance. Although this work deals primarily with events of the 1950s, it is of more than historical interest. Indeed, the information it provides makes it clear that the record of the past quarter century could easily have been predicted; the only novel quality is the ferocity with which the Zionist strategy of the fifties has been carried out in the decades that followed. No longer does the Zionist movement feel compelled to hide its true intentions. Its regional alliances with the Phalanges party and other right-wing elements in South Lebanon, and its special relationship with the United States, propel it like a juggernaut in pursuit of imperial goals.

The first edition of this book appeared when the Middle East and the United States were preoccupied with the Egyptian-Israeli negotiations that led to the 1978 Camp David Accords and the Egyptian-Israeli treaty of March 1979, and with the Israeli invasion of South Lebanon of March 1978. Subsequently, the Camp David formula not only has failed to produce the comprehensive settlement promised by President Jimmy Carter, it in fact contributed to a second Israeli invasion of Lebanon in June 1982. By neutralizing Egypt, the Egyptian-Israeli treaty allowed Israel to proceed confidently with its plans to crush Palestinian resistance and obliterate the Palestinian national identity, with a view to perpetuating its occupation of the West Bank, Gaza Strip and Golan Heights. Today, the Palestine question is further from a peaceful and just resolution than at any time in the past, while Lebanon continues to hemorrhage and to divide along sectarian lines.

The Camp David Accords, and the subsequent Reagan Plan introduced in September 1982, were grounded in flawed assumptions about Israel's "security" and Arab threats to that security. Recent developments in the region have exposed the Reagan administration's complicity in the 1982 Israeli invasion of Lebanon,[2] which was calculated to produce results deemed beneficial both to American strategic interests and to Israeli expansionist goals. The interests of the Reagan administration and Israel's Likud government coalesced around three objectives: the destruction of the Palestinian infrastructure in Lebanon, the redrawing of the political map in Lebanon, and the reduction of Syria to manageable proportions. *Pax Americana* and *pax Israelica* were to be realized through the campaign cynically dubbed "Peace for Galilee."

The 1982 "operation," as well as its predecessor, the "Litani Operation" of 1978, were part of the long-standing Zionist strategy for Lebanon and Palestine, which this translation of the Sharett diary illuminates. In fact, that strategy, formulated and applied during the 1950s, had been envisaged at least four decades earlier, and attempts to implement it are still being carried out three decades later. On November 6, 1918, a committee of British mandate officials and Zionist leaders put forth a suggested northern boundary for a Jewish Palestine "from the North Litani River up to Banias." In the following year, at the Paris peace conference, the Zionist movement proposed boundaries that would have included the Lebanese district of Bint Jubayl and all the territories up to the Litani River. The proposal emphasized the "vital importance of controlling all water resources up to their sources."

During the Paris conference, Chaim Weizmann and David Ben Gurion (who later became, respectively, Israel's first president and first prime minister) attempted to persuade Patriarch Hayik, who headed the Lebanese delegation, to abandon South Lebanon in return for a promise of technical and financial assistance to develop the area to the north, which they hoped, would become a Christian state.

The Zionist military forces that invaded Palestine in 1948 also occupied part of the district of Marjayun and Bint Jubayl, and reached the vicinity of the Litani River, but were forced to withdraw under international pressure. Then, in 1954, the leaders of the newly established state of Israel renewed Zionist claims on Lebanese water when President Eisenhower's envoy Eric Johnston proposed a formula of sharing the Litani waters among Lebanon, Syria and Israel. Israel, in fact, threatened to use force against Lebanon to prevent the utilization of the Litani waters to develop South Lebanon.

While these threats were made during the period covered in the Sharett diary, consider what actually happened later, during the 1960s, '70s, '80s: In 1967, Israel's war against three Arab states not only gave Israel possession of eastern Palestine (the West Bank), Gaza, the Sinai and the Syrian Golan Heights, but also enabled Israel to capture the headwaters of the Jordan and Banias rivers. In addition, Israel destroyed Jordan's East Ghor Canal and its Khaled Dam on the Yarmuk River, which flows into Israel's Nahariya Pool. In the 1978 "Litani Operation," Israel established firm control over the Wazzani River, which flows into the Jordan, as well as almost the entire length of the Hasbani River. And in the 1982 "Operation Peace for Galilee," the entire length of the Litani River came under Israeli control.[3]

The goal of profoundly altering water distribution in the region could be achieved only within the context of a vassal state in Lebanon with a puppet government, an endeavor about which the Sharett diary has much to say (p. 22 ff). In fact, Ben Gurion's plan, in 1954, to establish such a puppet government—a plan enthusiastically endorsed by Moshe Dayan—was finally put in motion nearly a quarter of a century later. Dayan's "officer" did indeed emerge, even bearing the same rank of "just a major"—Major Sa'd Haddad, whom Israel encouraged to proclaim secession from Lebanon in April 1979. Israel's defense minister, Ezer Weizmann, announced his government's support of Haddad's canton of "Free Lebanon": "I consider Haddad a Lebanese nationalist and as far as I know he wants Beirut to become the capital of a free independent Lebanon once more without interference from the Syrians or the Palestinians."[4] Support for Haddad, and by implication for a Zionist-Phalangist alliance, was also voiced by right-wing Lebanese politicians. Stated Camille Chamoun, "We need such a Lebanese force to struggle in the South for the liberation of Lebanon, and not just a part of Lebanon, and Sa'd Haddad is not a traitor."[5]

But the Zionist proxy "mini-state," which was set up in a border strip six miles wide and sixty miles long, was repudiated by the world community. A United Nations force, the United Nations Interim Force in Lebanon (UNIFIL), was mandated to help re-establish the authority of the central Lebanese government in the South. Israel, however, defied the relevant United Nations resolution (which was supported even by the Carter administration) and persisted in its support of Haddad. After a March 1981 agreement by the Syrian and Lebanese presidents to reassert, in cooperation with UNIFIL, the authority of the Beirut government in the South, Israel and Haddad's militia bombarded a UNIFIL position, killing three Nigerian soldiers (March 16, 1981).

Israel's destabilization of Lebanon, in pursuit of a Maronite-dominated client state, has taken several forms, ranging from extending the Camp David formula to Lebanon, to its full-scale invasion of 1982. With regard to imposing a Camp David solution on Lebanon, Menachem Begin made a statement to the Israeli parliament on May 7, 1979, inviting Lebanon to enter into negotiations with Israel on the basis of Syrian withdrawal and expulsion of the Palestinians from Lebanon. This proposal evoked an enthusiastic response from Bashir Gemayel, commander of the Phalangist Lebanese Forces, who told Beirut's *Monday Morning* on May 28, 1979: "These principles are sound and should be accepted as the basis for any Lebanese endeavor to find a solution.... President Sadat accepted a similar proposal and he is now leading Egypt to an era of welfare and prosperity. When shall Lebanon be allowed the right to seek its own welfare?" The elder Gemayel, Pierre, added: "You shall say that I am defending Sadat as I defended Sa'd Haddad; my dear, I would be a coward and without honor if I did not defend my point of view" (*Al-Safir*, August 2, 1979).

Israel's aggression against Lebanon in 1982 was clearly designed to cement these alliances between Israel and the "Major" in the South and with the Gemayels and Chamouns to the North—all in an effort to secure the balkanization and vassalization of Lebanon, the eradication of Palestinian nationalism, and the intimidation of Syria. To attain these goals, Israeli leaders were willing to risk a wider regional war, and indeed to push the world to what is in every respect a "pre-nuclear" situation. This alone should give the American people cause for concern and action. In addition, the United States has provided Israel with the economic and military means to invade Lebanon, to bomb Baghdad, and to perpetuate the occupation of Palestine and of Syrian territory in clear violation of U.S. law, including the Arms Export Control Act of 1976 and the Israel-U.S. Mutual Defense Agreement of 1952.

The 1982 Israeli invasion so tipped the domestic balance in favor of Israel's Lebanese allies that the majority of Muslims, nationalists and other anti-Israel groups were left in a clearly submissive condition. The terms of the victor were dictated to the vanquished. Israel's new ally, Bashir Gemayel, was to be president/viceroy of Lebanon, although according to noted American journalist Jonathan Randal, Bashir himself, who owed his presidency to Begin and Sharon, complained that these two treated him like a "vassal."[6] The Shultz agreement of May 17, 1983 was to be Lebanon's Versailles, which would realize the long-standing Zionist dream described in the Sharett diaries—a "Christian" state that would ally itself with Israel.

Despite the assassination of President-elect Bashir Gemayel before he could take office, initially matters developed in accordance with Israel's strategy for Lebanon. The negotiations, handled by civilians from the two countries' foreign ministries, appeared to be headed towards normalization along Camp David lines; Israel secured a liaison office in Beirut, the next thing to an embassy; the Phalanges party and its leader's son, Amin Gemayel, now the president of Lebanon, began to reshape the country in their own image. But it soon became clear that sectarian hegemony, sponsored by Israel and supported by the United States, was a poor substitute for even the antiquated confessional system of 1943. By fall 1983, Israeli troops were forced to withdraw to the Awali River. By February 1984, President Reagan ordered U.S. troops to withdraw, while Druze and Shiite fighters made a triumphant entry into Beirut (February 10, 1984). President Amin Gemayel, who owed his presidency to the Israeli invasion, was forced under new political and military conditions to repudiate the Shultz agreement (March 1984) and to close Israel's "embassy" in Beirut (July of the same year).

Not only did the Israeli invasion of 1982 fail to achieve most of its objectives: It pushed the right-wing Lebanese Forces to a position that borders on fascism and renders reunification and reintegration a remote possibility. It has exacerbated the Lebanese civil war at an unbearable cost in human lives and property.

This human tragedy compels us to examine the Israeli rationale of "security," a rubric that has covered a curiously large number of Israeli violations of international law and human rights, recently and in the past. Why, we must ask, does Israel in the West Bank and Gaza Strip close universities, shoot students in classrooms and on the street, deport leaders, dismiss mayors, create colonial settlements and encourage terrorist acts by settlers—all in the name of "security?" Why, when confronted with massive popular resistance to its occupation of South Lebanon, did Israel react with the same "Iron Fist," initiating raids on villages, mass arrests of civilians, wide-scale destruction of homes and property, and assassinations—even though this policy could only further alienate the population?

The personal diary of Moshe Sharett sheds light on this question by amply documenting the rationale and mechanics of Israel's "Arab policy" in the late 1940s and the 1950s. The policy portrayed, in its most intimate particulars, is one of deliberate Israeli acts of provocation, intended to generate Arab hostility and thus to create pretexts for armed action and territorial expansion. Sharett's records document this policy of "sacred terrorism" and expose the myths of Israel's "security needs" and the "Arab threat" that have been treated like self-evident truths from the creation of Israel to the present, when Israeli terrorism against Palestinians in the West Bank and Gaza Strip, and against Palestinians and Lebanese in South Lebanon, has reached an intolerable level. It is becoming increasingly evident that the exceptional demographic and geographic alterations in Israeli society within the present generation have been brought about, not as the accidental results of the endeavor to guard "Israel's security" against an "Arab threat," but by a drive for *lebensraum.*

Referring to the terrorist bombings that crippled two prominent West Bank mayors and injured other civilians on June 2, 1980, William Browder, in an article for the *New York Times* (June 5, 1980), explained the apprehension of West Bank Palestinians: "...although military occupation is not new to them, Israeli terrorism—if that is what it was—is virtually without precedent in the last thirty years." It behooves Mr. Browder and the attentive public who reads the "news that's fit to print," to examine the many precedents—amply documented and occasionally decried by a bewildered Israeli prime minister who worried about the moral deterioration in Israeli society in the 1950s—that first prompted revenge as a "sacred" principle. In a passage quoted in Rokach's study,

Sharett wrote: "In the thirties we restrained the emotions of revenge.... Now, on the contrary, we justify the system of reprisal...we have eliminated the mental and moral brake on this instinct and made it possible...to uphold revenge as a moral value... a sacred principle" (p. 33).

The undisguised satisfaction that the maiming of the two Palestinian mayors evoked among many Jewish settlers in the West Bank is reminiscent of the feeling in Israel in the 1950s that caused Sharett so much anguish, and challenged his conscience. In fact, the private armies now being organized by Jewish vigilante groups determined to keep the occupied West Bank and Gaza Strip under permanent Israeli control, have openly advocated the removal of all Arabs from occupied Palestine. Although these ultra-nationalists consider former Prime Minister Menachem Begin and Foreign Minister Yitzhak Shamir (former members of the terrorist Irgun and Stern gangs) to have become patsies, fools and traitors, and although Begin condemned the attacks on the Palestinian mayors as "crimes of the worst kind," the fact remains that the settlers of Gush Emunim and Kach are carrying out the settlement policies of the Israeli government. This government provides them with the protection and economic benefits and equips them with legitimacy. By the same token, it ensures that their victims will be defenseless and powerless. The 1948 Deir Yassin massacre, committed by Begin's Irgun Zvei Leumi, and the June 2, 1980 bombing, committed by another vigilante group, are products of the same type of "sacred terrorism."

The thirty-two years that have lapsed in the interim have witnessed innumerable acts of Israeli terror: it hardly seems necessary to recall the aerial bombardment of vital civilian infrastructures in Egypt and Syria in the late 1960s,[7] or the destruction of southern Lebanon in the 1970s and '80s, nor to mention the brutality with which the occupation regime treats the Palestinians in the West Bank and Gaza, or the many assassinations of Palestinian intellectuals in various European capitals in the early 1970s.

A most disturbing phenomenon, which will continue to inhibit the prospects for Palestinian-Israeli coexistence, is the ascendancy of the radical right in Israel. Its orientation towards brute force, its attitude towards Arabs, and its contempt for debate and dissent, leave little room for coexistence. Justifications of acts of terrorism against Palestinian civilians are rampant among members of the political establishment and Jewish settlers. Israel's former Minister of Science and Energy, Yuval Neeman, Knesset member Haim Druckman, former chief of staff Raphael Eytan, and Sephardic chief Rabbi Mordechai Eliahu are on record justifying that kind of terrorism.[8] In July 1985, Foreign Minister Yitzhak Shamir vowed to work for the early release of convicted Jewish terrorists, whom he described as "excellent people who made a mistake" (*Jerusalem Post*, July 12, 1985). The propensity for violence against

Arabs has been clearly established in interviews of settlers, young and old, by Israeli and Western journalists.[9]

The radical right nowadays speaks outright of dispossession and deportation of Palestinians. Israeli sociologist Yoram Peri wrote in *Davar* (May 11, 1984) that while Defense Minister Arens and Foreign Minister Shamir speak of annexing the West Bank and Gaza and forging a "pluralistic" society, the extreme right advocates deportation, a term which, four years ago, no one would dare utter. "Hence," he wrote, "the proximity of the right to the Fascist conception of the State."

Another factor that inhibits coexistence is the cavalier manner in which members of the establishment claim sovereignty over the West Bank and Gaza. So contemptuous of the need to argue and convince was Foreign Minister Shamir, that his reply to a question of why Israel lay claims to those territories consisted of one word: "Because!" Israel's Chief Rabbi, Shlomo Goren, has remarked that in religious law retaining the occupied territories takes precedence over the duty to save life. Terms such as "Western Eretz Israel" and "Judea and Samaria," which are being used with more frequency and emphasis, represent a revival of the revisionist Zionist notion that the "land of Israel" also includes modern-day Jordan, and underline Israeli leaders' determination never to relinquish the illegally occupied West Bank and Gaza Strip.

The more the world tries to understand the situation in the Middle East, the more the Zionist organizations in the United States, acting in concert with Israel, try to fog it up. Israel's wars against the Arabs in 1967 and 1982 obliterated its David image and confirmed it as the Goliath of the Middle East. No longer was it possible for the Israeli government to escape public scrutiny, despite all the immunity which it enjoys in the American public arena, as its forces, in the name of "security" for Israeli civilians, carried out the most ruthless aerial bombardment since Vietnam. The U.S. ambassador in Lebanon, whose government used its Security Council veto to protest Israel's war gains in 1982, described their saturation bombing: "There is no pinpoint accuracy against targets in open spaces." The Canadian ambassador said Israel's bombing "would make Berlin of 1944 look like a tea party...it is truly a scene from Dante's Inferno." NBC's John Chancellor said: "I kept thinking of the bombing of Madrid during the Spanish Civil War...we are now dealing with an imperial Israel." Indeed, in their pure murderousness, given the frequent use of phosphorus and cluster bombs, the Israeli bombings of Beirut, an advanced form of state terrorism, far outstripped the attacks on Guernica, Coventry and Dresden.

Since this book was first published in 1980, the Zionist movement has responded to the growing criticism of Israeli violence in a hysterical manner. Surveillance, monitoring the activities of Israel's critics in the media, churches and on the campus, intelligence gathering and black-listing reminiscent of the McCarthy period in the United States, are among the tactics employed recently by Zionist organizations to stifle criticism of Israel.[10] Pinning the anti-Semitic label on critics has become the standard and easiest tactic to pre-empt rational discussion of public policy regarding Israel and to intimidate would-be critics. The list of victims includes such distinguished individuals as former Senator Charles Percy, the Reverend Jesse Jackson, former Under Secretary of State George Ball, former Congressman Paul Findley,[11] and many other lesser known individuals who struggle against overwhelming odds to retain a job and secure their livelihood. Menachem Begin's famous remark after the Sabra and Shatila massacres, which defined criticism of Israel as "blood libel against the Jewish people," is a stark example of the trend to equate open criticism with anti-Semitism, even as Israel continues to have trade relations and military cooperation with the most notoriously anti-Semitic regimes in Central and South America.[12] Israel's war against journalists was revealed in the legal suit against NBC's reporting of the 1982 invasion of Lebanon,[13] its repeated allegations that journalists who report news detrimental to Israel do so only in response to Arab "threats,"[14] and in the killing of CBS crewmen in South Lebanon, who were covering the implementation of Israel's "Iron Fist" policy (March 21, 1985).

Other hysterical responses to increasing knowledge of the facts of the Middle East conflict have emerged in the writings of propagandists masquerading as scholars. Joan Peters's *From Time Immemorial*[15] turns history on its head by claiming that Jews did not replace native Palestinians, who were allegedly no more than illegal Arab immigrant workers who moved to "where they found work." The absurd and indefensible allegation that there were virtually no Arabs in Palestine prior to the Zionist influx, seems intended to provide a veneer of legitimacy for Israel's increasingly violent efforts to make the myth that there is "no such thing as a Palestinian" a chilling reality.

The Zionist effort to stifle public debate of Israeli actions extended to the present study. After unsuccessful attempts by the Israeli establishment to suppress publication, in Hebrew, of the Sharett diary in Israel, attempts were made—by threats of litigation and otherwise—to suppress our publication of this study of the diary here in the United States. On April 11, 1980 the AAUG received communication from a well-known law firm in New York requesting in the "firmest manner possible" that we refrain from printing, publishing or otherwise reproducing portions of the diary. The law firm, acting on behalf of the family of the late Moshe Sharett and the Israeli publisher of the diary, threatened to "initiate prompt litigation in a Federal District Court" on the grounds of alleged violation of United States copyright laws.

Subsequently, the AAUG received a telegram from the Sharett family emphasizing that all rights would be vigorously protected if the association published "parts or all of Moshe Sharett's diaries." Anxious transoceanic calls were received by our office from the Israeli media. Our right to publish was questioned, but not on the legal grounds cited by the Sharett family and its legal counsel. Instead, we were hysterically accused of attempting to expose Israel via Sharett in a sensationalist manner. The Israeli newspaper *Ma'ariv* headlined a front-page story, "Israel's Haters in the U.S.A. Translated with No Permission the Diaries of Moshe Sharett" (April 4, 1980). According to former Knesset member Uri Avneri, writing in *Haolam Hazeh* (September 23, 1980), the Israeli Foreign Ministry initially supported Moshe Sharett's son, Yaqov, who edited the Hebrew publication of the diary, in his attempt to suppress publication of Livia Rokach's study based on the diary. "But to his disappointment, the Foreign Office did not uphold its support for him. The Jerusalem politicians decided that pursuing a legal course in stopping the dissemination of the book would be a mistake of the first order, since this would give it much more publicity."

Needless to say, our accusers not only prejudged our book before its publication and cast aspersion on the organization and the individuals involved in its production; they also assumed that our publication was an unauthorized translation. In fact, the material quoted as verbatim translations from the Sharett diary or substantially paraphrased from that diary comprises only about one percent of the diary. Rokach's study utilizes excerpts from the Sharett diary to reinforce and illustrate her own thesis.

We are under no illusion that the challenge before us was predominantly legal. After all, what Sharett said in his diary, limited as it is to the Hebrew-speaking public, is very revealing; it constitutes an indictment of Zionism by the former prime minister of Israel, and dismantles many erroneous assumptions about the Arab-Israeli conflict. It refutes a three-decade-old dogma and emphasizes the need to re-examine the uncritical support Israel has enjoyed in the West for its policies toward the Arabs. Hence, the Israelis' need to suppress and censor, to withhold relevant and vital information from the public discourse on the Middle East. We are painfully reminded of similar attempts to conceal the fraudulent methods which the United States politico-military establishment employed in its pursuit of the war against the Vietnamese. The ability of the establishment to withhold the truth from the American public prolonged the Vietnam War and aggravated the social, economic, and human problems which resulted from that war. It will be hoped that the deceptive strategy of David Ben Gurion, which Moshe Sharett documented in his day-to-day record, will not be withheld forever from the American public, whose lives are materially affected by events in the Middle East. Thus, in our opinion, *Israel's Sacred Terrorism* has an indisputable significance in the formulation of a healthy and objective policy towards the Middle East.

It is our considered opinion that Sharett's *Personal Diary* is a very important historical resource that sheds much light on Israel's policy towards the Arab world, particularly for all of us in the United States who have such a large stake in Middle Eastern developments and the eventual outcome of the conflict. Therefore, the use of Sharett's historical resource for scholarly study does not infringe the copyright laws.

We have taken particular precautions, however, to ensure that our selections have been translated accurately, have not been taken out of context and are not mitigated or contradicted by anything that Sharett wrote elsewhere in the diary. We are also certain that these selections satisfy the "fair use" criteria of United States copyright law:

1. The AAUG is a non-profit, educational organization, which is not publishing this study for commercial exploitation.
2. The nature of Moshe Sharett's diary relates materially to the "right of the public to know."
3. The amount of the copyrighted material reproduced in this publication amounts to no more than one percent of the whole.
4. The economic value of the original work would not suffer from the limited quotations included in our study.

We take comfort in the protection afforded by the First Amendment to the United States Constitution involving freedom of speech and the press and the companion "right of the public to know." The Pentagon Papers were revealed to the public after they had long lain unnoticed in the archives of the American military bureaucracy. The critical nature of their content warranted that they should have been unearthed much earlier than their dramatic appearance. Sharett's startling revelations must not be subjected to the same bureaucratic strangulation, or kept away from the English-reading public so that their usefulness as a factor in Middle East policy is nullified.

NASEER H. ARURI
AAUG Publications Committee
November 1985

NOTES

1. Moshe Sharett, *Yoman Ishi* (Personal Diary), edited by Yaqov Sharett (Tel Aviv: Ma'a 1979).
2. For example, upon his retirement in May 1985, U.S. Ambassador to Israel Samuel Lewis revealed that in December 1981 Israeli Defense Minister Ariel Sharon outlined his plans for the impending invasion to U.S. envoy Philip Habib (*Washington Post*, 24 May 1985).

3. See for example Thomas Stauffer, "Israel Calculates the Price of Peace: Money and Water," *Christian Science Monitor*, 13 January 1982, and "Israel's Water Needs May Erode Path to Peace in Region," *Christian Science Monitor*, 20 January 1982; John Cooley, "Syria Links Pull-Out to Guaranteed Access to Water," *Washington Post*, 8 June 1983; and Leslie C. Schmida, "Israel's Drive for Water," *Link*, 17, 4 (November 1984).

4. Quoted in *al-Nahar* and *al-Safir*, 22 April 1979.

5. Quoted in *The Isolationist-Israeli Alliance Is a Phenomenon that Threatens the Unity of Lebanon*, presented at the World Congress for Solidarity with the Lebanese People, Paris, 16–18 June 1980 (Beirut: Information Bureau of the Lebanese National Movement, 1980), 9.

6. Jonathan C. Randal, *Going All the Way: Christian Warlords, Israeli Adventurers, and the War in Lebanon* (New York: Viking Press, 1983), 10–11.

7. In the late 1960s and the early 1970s, Israeli bombing reduced the Egyptian cities of Suez, Port Said and Ismailia to ghost towns. During the same period Israel carried out repeated air raids against Syria. Following the killing of eleven Israeli athletes at the Munich Olympics in 1972, at least 200 people, almost all civilians, were killed in Israeli "reprisal" raids in Syria alone. David Hirst, *The Gun and the Olive Branch* (London: Futura, 1978), 251–252.

8. See articles by Yoram Peri in *Davar*, 11 May 1984. Ya'acov Rahamim in *Ma'ariv*, 14 December 1983, and Mary Curtius, "Israeli Debate: Should Settlers Be Pardoned," *Christian Science Monitor*, 15 July 1985.

9. See, for example, *Christian Science Monitor*, 10 May 1984.

10. At its annual convention in 1984, the Middle East Studies Association called on the American Israel Public Affairs Committee (AIPAC) and the Anti-Defamation League of B'nai B'rith to "disavow and refrain from" blacklisting practices against scholars and students. For more information on efforts by supporters of Israel to quash open debate, see, for example, Naseer Aruri, "The Middle East on the U.S. Campus," *Link*, 18, 2 (May–June 1985).

11. Former Congressman Findley documents the pervasive influence of the American Israel Public Affairs Committee (AIPAC) in *They Dare to Speak Out* (Westport, Conn.: Lawrence Hill, 1985).

12. For a detailed analysis of Israel's relations with Central American regimes, see Milton Jamail and Margo Gutierrez, *It's No Secret: Israel's Military Involvement in Central America*, forthcoming, AAUG. See also Israel Shahak, *Israel's Global Role: Weapons for Repression* (Belmont, Mass.: AAUG, 1982).

13. In May 1984 a pro-Israel group known as Americans for a Safe Israel (AFSI) filed a petition with the Federal Communications Commission to deny renewal of licenses for station WNBC-TV in New York and seven other NBC affiliates, charging that NBC had presented one-sided coverage of the war in Lebanon. See *Christian Science Monitor*, 14 May 1984. AFSI also commissioned Professor Edward Alexander to write a study, which appeared under the title *NBC's War In Lebanon: The Distorting Mirror* (1983).

14. An example is Ze'ev Chafets, *Double Vision: How the Press Distorts America's View of the Middle East* (New York: William Morrow, 1983). Chafets is former head of the Israeli press office in Jerusalem. American journalists have vigorously denied these allegations. (See, e.g., Charles Glass, ABC Beirut correspondent, in *CPJ Update* [published by the Committee to Protect Journalists], November–December 1984).

15. New York: Harper and Row, 1984. For critical reviews of Peter's book, see Norman Finklestein, in *In These Times*, 5–11 September 1984, 12–13; Muhammad Hallaj, *"From Time Immemorial:* The Resurrection of a Myth," *Link*, 18, 1 (January–March 1985); and Ian Gilmour and David Gilmour, in *Arab Studies Quarterly*, 7, 2–3 (Spring/Summer 1985), 181–195.

INTRODUCTION———————————————————

   Popular Western support of Israel over the last quarter of a century has been based on a number of myths, the most persistent of which has been the myth of Israel's security. Implying the permanent existence of grave threats to the survival of Jewish society in Palestine, this myth has been carefully cultivated to evoke anxious images in public opinion to permit, and even encourage, the use of large amounts of public funds to sustain Israel militarily and economically. "Israel's security" is the official argument with which not only Israel but also the U.S. denies the right of self-determination in their own country to the Palestinian people. For the past three decades it has been accepted as a legitimate explanation for Israel's violation of international resolutions calling for the return of the Palestinian people to their homes. Over the past thirteen years Israel has been allowed to evoke its security to justify its refusal to retreat from the Arab and Palestinian territories occupied in 1967. Security is still the pretext given by successive Israeli governments for widespread massacres of civilian populations in Lebanon, for expropriations of Arab lands, for the establishment of Jewish settlements in the occupied territories, for deportations, and for arbitrary detentions of political prisoners. Although the security of the Arab populations in the whole region has been repeatedly threatened over these years by overt and covert warfare, terrorist plots and subversive designs, and although UN resolutions demand the establishment of secure borders for *all* states in the region, so far only Israel's security has been at the center of international discussion.
   The persistence of the myth of Israel's security shows that there is considerable public belief in the so-called Arab commitment to eliminate the Jewish state. Most of the distinguished Western writers who present this case derive their arguments from Zionist versions of events in the late 1940s, at the time of the establishment of Israel, and in the mid-1950s, when Nasser came to power. They go on from these arguments to present Israel's so-called struggle for security and survival as a *moral* issue. The media often furnish politicians, who have *other* reasons for their political and military support of Israel, with the convenient issue of the West's moral commitment to Israel.
   Other versions or approaches to the facts have more often than not been ignored. For example, recent disclosures by Nahum Goldmann *(Le Monde Diplomatique*, August 1979) have gone practically unnoticed.

Goldmann, who for more than thirty years headed the pro-Zionist World Jewish Congress, charges that the Arabs were not consulted about the partition of Palestine in 1947, and further that their willingness to negotiate a political compromise that might have prevented the 1948 war was vetoed and undermined by Ben Gurion before May 1948.

The recently published *Personal Diary* of Moshe Sharett (*Yoman Ishi*. Tel Aviv: Ma'ariv, 1979, in Hebrew) now offers a decisive and authoritative contribution to the demystification of the myth of Israel's security and its security policies. Between 1933 and 1948 Sharett guided the foreign relations of the Zionist movement, as head of the Jewish Agency's Political Department, and from 1948 to 1956 he was Israel's foreign minister. In 1954 and 1955 he was its prime minister as well. The following pages present extracts from Sharett's diary demonstrating the following points:

1. The Israeli political/military establishment never seriously believed in an Arab threat to the existence of Israel. On the contrary, it sought and applied every means to exacerbate the dilemma of the Arab regimes after the 1948 war. The Arab governments were extremely reluctant to engage in any military confrontation with Israel, yet in order to survive they needed to project to their populations—and to the exiled Palestinians in their countries—some kind of reaction to Israel's aggressive policies and continuous acts of harassment. In other words, the Arab threat was an Israeli-invented myth which for internal and inter-Arab reasons the Arab regimes could not completely deny, though they constantly feared Israeli preparations for a new war.

2. The Israeli political/military establishment aimed at pushing the Arab states into military confrontations which the Israeli leaders *were invariably certain of winning*. The goal of these confrontations was to modify the balance of power in the region radically, transforming the Zionist state into *the* major power in the Middle East.

3. In order to achieve this strategic purpose the following tactics were used:

   a) Large- and small-scale military operations aimed at civilian populations across the armistice lines, especially in the Palestinian territories of the West Bank and Gaza, then respectively under the control of Jordan and Egypt. These operations had a double purpose: to terrorize the populations, and to create a permanent destabilization stemming from tensions between the Arab governments and the populations, who felt they were not adequately protected against Israeli aggression.

   b) Military operations against Arab military installations in border areas to undermine the morale of the armies and intensify the regimes' destabilization from inside their military structures.

   c) Covert terrorist operations in depth inside the Arab world, used for both espionage and to create fear, tension and instability.

4. Israel's achievement of its strategic purpose was to be realized through

the following means:

a) New territorial conquests through war. Although the 1949-50 armistice agreements assigned to Israel a territory one-third larger than had the UN partition plan, the Israeli leadership was still not satisfied with the size of the state, the borders of which it had committed itself to respect on the international level. It sought to recover *at least* the borders of mandate Palestine. The territorial dimension was considered to be a vital factor in Israel's transformation into a regional power.

b) Political as well as military efforts to bring about the liquidation of all Arab and Palestinian claims to Palestine through the dispersion of the Palestinian refugees of the 1947-49 war to faraway parts of the Arab world as well as outside the Arab world[1]

c) Subversive operations designed to dismember the Arab world, defeat the Arab national movement, and create puppet regimes which would gravitate to the regional Israeli power.

In providing documentation on the above points, Sharett's *Diary* deals a deadly blow to a number of important interpretations which are still being presented as historical truths. Among these are the following items:

1. To this date the majority of scholars and analysts cite the nationalization of the Suez Canal as the chief motivation for the October 1956 war. It is thereby implied that the projected British and French aggression against Egypt provided Israel with an opportunity to achieve the termination of fedayeen attacks from across the armistice lines, and to settle its accounts with Nasser's regime, to which these attacks were attributed.

What Sharett tells us now is that a major war against Egypt aimed at the territorial conquest of Gaza and the Sinai was on the Israeli leadership's agenda at least as early as the *autumn of 1953*, almost a year before Nasser ousted Neguib and consolidated his leadership. It was agreed then that the international conditions for such a war would mature within a period of about three years. The Israeli military attack on Gaza in February 1955 was consciously undertaken as a preliminary act of war. A couple of months later a government decision to commence a war to conquer the Gaza Strip met with the strenuous opposition of the foreign minister, whose political liquidation was thereupon decided by the supporters of the war policy, headed by Ben Gurion. Had the prospect of the tripartite aggression not appeared on the horizon in later months, Israel would have gone on to attack Egypt according to its own plans, and, moreover, with U.S. consent.

2. The occupation by Israel of the West Bank and Gaza in 1967 has been described, and is still widely understood today, as an Israeli defensive action in the face of Arab threats. Sharett's *Diary* offers unequivocable evidence that the occupation of Gaza and also of the West Bank was part of Israel's plans since the early fifties. American Zionist leaders

were informed about these plans in 1954. In 1955, Jewish and Arab lives were sacrificed in a series of provocative attacks undertaken to create a pretext for the occupation of Jordanian territory. The chief obstacle postponing this occupation was Britain's residual presence in Jordan upholding the Hashemite throne.

3. The continuing, violent Israeli aggression in Lebanon still is being attributed, shamelessly, to Israeli security needs. In particular, Israeli spokesmen, echoed by Western media, try to explain Israel's massive intervention in Lebanon and the Lebanese events in general, with the following historical arguments:

   a) In the struggle between Muslims and Christians, a conflict which would have broken out regardless of outside interference, Israel's role has been limited to the defense of the Christian minority.

   b) The presence of the Palestinian resistance, or in Israeli terminology, of Palestinian terrorism in that country required Israeli intervention.

Sharett's *Diary*, however, provides the entire documentation of how in 1954 Ben Gurion developed the diabolic plans to "Christianize" Lebanon, i.e., to invent and create from scratch the inter-Lebanese conflict, and of how a detailed blueprint for the partition and subordination of that country to Israel was elaborated by Israel more than fifteen years before the Palestinian presence became a political factor in Lebanon.

The use of terror and aggression to provoke or create the appearance of an Arab threat to Israel's existence was summed up by the then "number two" of the Zionist state's hierarchy:

> I have been meditating on the long chain of false incidents and hostilities we have invented, and on the many clashes we have provoked which cost us so much blood, and on the violations of the law by our men—all of which brought grave disasters and determined the whole course of events and contributed to the security crisis.

A week earlier, Moshe Dayan, then Israel's chief of staff, explained why Israel needed to reject any border security arrangements offered by the neighboring Arab states, or by the United Nations, as well as the formal security guarantees suggested by the United States. Such guarantees, he predicted, might "tie Israel's hands." Presumably, that would render unjustifiable or even impossible those attacks and incursions across the armistice lines which through the mid-1950s went under the euphemistic name of reprisal actions. These actions, Dayan said,

> are our vital lymph. They . . . help us maintain a high tension among our population and in the army . . . in order to have young men go to the Negev we have to cry out that it is in danger. (26 May 1955, 1021)

The creation of a siege mentality in Israeli society was necessary to complement the prefabricated myth of the Arab threat. The two elements were intended to feed each other. Although Israeli society faced a serious risk of social and cultural disintegration under the impact of a mass immigration of Asian and North African Jews into the pre-state's ideologically homogeneous community, the purpose of the siege mentality was not so much that of attaining a defensive cohesiveness in Israel's Jewish society. It was calculated principally to "eliminate the moral brakes" required for a society to fully support a policy which constituted a complete reversal of the collective ethical code on which its formal education was based and from which it was supposed to derive its vital strength. Of course, this ethical code had not been respected in the past either. Aggression and terrorism had been exercised by the Zionists before and during the 1947-48 war. The following testimony of a soldier who participated in the occupation of the Palestinian village of Dueima in 1948 is only the most recently disclosed of a long chain of evidence:

> Killed between 80 to 100 Arabs, women and children. To kill the children they fractured their heads with sticks. There was not one house without corpses. The men and women of the villages were pushed into houses without food or water. Then the saboteurs came to dynamite the houses. One commander ordered a soldier to bring two women into a house he was about to blow up. . . . Another soldier prided himself upon having raped an Arab woman before shooting her to death. Another Arab woman with her newborn baby was made to clean the place for a couple of days, and then they shot her and the baby. Educated and well-mannered commanders who were considered "good guys" . . . became base murderers, and this not in the storm of battle, but as a method of expulsion and extermination. The fewer the Arabs who remain, the better. (quoted in *Davar*, 9 June 1979)

But these episodes did not filter through to the society at large. The War of Independence was ritualized, on the contrary, as a miraculous victory of (Jewish) right against (Arab) might. Deir Yassin was (falsely) described by the ruling Labor establishment as an isolated and even condemnable case, a product of the brutality of the minority Irgun group. Manuals, school textbooks, history books, anthologies and the media placidly glorified the moral quality of the war, the "purity of the weapons" used by the army, the Jewish ethos underlying the state.

The security or reprisals policy of the 1950s represented, in this sense, a qualitative leap. The strategic designs were perceived, by the Israeli leaders themselves, as totally irrational in respect to the regional realities, and especially in respect to the international context to which Israel had formally committed itself. Therefore, the support required for it inside the country had to be total, i.e., emotional, almost instinctive, with no concessions to rationality and no moralistic cover. A strategic goal such as the transformation of Israel into a regional power *inevitably* presupposed the use of large-scale, open violence, and could not pretend even mythically to be achieved on the basis of the earlier moral superiority doctrine which, therefore, had to be replaced with a new one. Terrorism and "revenge" were now to be glorified as the new *"moral . . . and even sacred"* values of Israeli society. The resurgent militarism no longer needed the idealistic, socialist varnish of a Palmach: the military symbol was now Unit 101, led by Arik Sharon.

The process of this cultural even more than political transition was not automatic. In fact, as Dayan admitted in the above quotation, much anxiety had to be generated to encourage it. The lives of Jewish victims also had to be sacrificed to create provocations justifying subsequent reprisals, especially in those periods in which the Arab governments succeeded in controlling the reactions of the harassed and enraged Arab border populations. A hammering, daily propaganda, controlled by the censors, was directed to feed the Israeli population with images of the monstrosity of the Enemy. More images showed that negotiated security arrangements with the Enemy could only be interpreted as a fatal proof of Israeli weakness.

The final point of this process which Sharett watched in the 1950s was the election of Menachem Begin as prime minister in 1977. Sharett's Zionist perspective was based on a political/diplomatic alternative to the terror strategy of Ben Gurion and his followers. This, he thought, could consolidate the establishment of a Jewish state in Palestine and perhaps enlarge it in the future, without major concessions to the surrounding Arab world. Sharett believed his goals could be achieved without disturbing the West. Indeed, he thought Israeli plans could be coordinated with the West's. He lucidly perceived as fascist the logic behind Israel's security doctrine, and correctly evaluated its consequences of moral corruption on the internal level and increasing violence on the regional level. He opposed it, and was certainly its most illustrious victim. His defeat, however, was inevitable, because his dissent from the strategy was quantitative more than qualitative: on methods rather than substance; on the number, for example, of the victims of a given military action and only vaguely on the ideology behind such actions. Basically, in the light of his unflagging Zionist faith, he was as fascinated as repelled by the strategy, as envious of its immediate successes as he was worried over its longer range consequences and international repercussions for Zionism and Israel.

The liquidation of his dissenting presence was considered indispensable to the realization of the Israeli political/military leadership's megalomaniac and criminal designs. His intrinsic weakness consisted in his *seemingly* rational hope that the so-called liberal West would prevent the implementation of his opponents' designs. He relied on the West rather than on the awakening of a local, popular conscience which he had the power and the information to provoke but which as a Zionist he could not and dared not do.

On the contrary, notwithstanding his scruples and torments he almost invariably ended up collaborating with his adversaries, and with those elements in the security establishment who conspired against him, in the fabrication and diffusion of deliberately distorted versions of events and policies for domestic and international consumption.

In a historical perspective Sharett's self-portrait as it emerges from his *Personal Diary* thus also explains why no so-called moderate Zionist proposal is possible, and how any attempt to liberalize Zionism from the inside could not but—as has repeatedly been the case—end in defeat. A clear, lucid, coherent logic runs through the history of the past three decades. In the early fifties the bases were laid for constructing a state imbued with the principles of *sacred terrorism* against the surrounding Arab societies; on the threshold of the eighties the same state is for the first time denounced by its own intellectuals as being tightly in the deadly grip of fascism.

This may be just one more reason why Western journalists, scholars and analysts may find themselves greatly embarrassed by the following document. These commentators still insist on upholding the presumed moral commitment of the West to what they obstinately continue to mystify as Israel's security. In this sense Sharett's *Diary* is potentially devastating to Zionist propaganda as the Pentagon Papers were in regard to U.S. aggression in Vietnam.

1

Moshe Sharett
and His Personal Diary _____

Moshe Sharett (Shertok) was born in Harsson, Russia, in 1894. He emigrated with his family—his father was a fervent Zionist activist—to Palestine in 1906, at the age of twelve. The family settled in the Arab village of Ein Sinya, near Nablus. Later, Moshe, his brother and three sisters would describe that two-year period, during which they studied Arabic, played with the children of the village and learned fascinating stories from the village's elders as the happiest time of their lives.

In 1908 the Shertok family moved to Tel Aviv, where Moshe entered the Hertselyah High School. At the outbreak of World War I, he was conscripted into the Ottoman army, where he took an officer's course and then served as an officer, mostly in Syria. After the war, while the British Mandate was established in Palestine, he graduated from the London School of Economics, and shortly thereafter entered political activity in the ranks of Labor Zionism. He was a founding member of Mapai (Party of the Workers of Eretz Israel), and became chief editor of *Davar*, the daily organ of the Histadrut (the trade union federation dominated by Mapai). Later he was appointed as deputy to Haim Arlosorov, the head of the Jewish Agency's Political Department. After Arlosorov was murdered on a Tel Aviv beach in 1933, Sharett was appointed as his successor. The Chairman of the Jewish Agency at that time was David Ben Gurion.

According to Sharett, the conflict with Ben Gurion which characterized their twenty-five years of close collaboration at the summit of the Zionist movement and the state of Israel, originated in suspicions on Ben Gurion's part that Sharett was loyal to Chaim Weizmann, the president of the World Zionist Organization. In the 1940s Ben Gurion accused Sharett, unjustly according to the latter, of collaborating with Weizmann to negotiate, with U.S. mediation, an agreement between the Zionist movement and the Emir Faisal of Saudi Arabia. Sharett claimed that in reality he contributed to the failure of those negotiations. But according to Dr. Nahum Goldmann, Sharett was again involved in 1947-48 with Goldmann in negotiations mediated by U.S. Secretary of State George Marshall, aimed at obtaining a political solution to the problem of the Zionist presence in Palestine, possibly leading to creating a Middle Eastern Confederation including a Zionist entity. The main negotiator on the Arab side was to be Egyptian Foreign Minister Nukrashi Pasha. These negotiations, which were expected to prevent the first Arab-Israeli war, would have meant postponing the date scheduled for the proclamation of the state of Israel by a few weeks. Ben Gurion vetoed the negotiations, rejected the postponement, and accused Sharett of being opposed to the creation of the state, an accusation he vehemently denied. Fundamentally, Ben Gurion's preference for the use of force, versus Sharett's preference for the diplomatic method to achieve the same goals, was the basis for the conflict between these two Zionist leaders, which lasted until Sharett was ousted from the Israeli government in June 1956. Moshe Sharett died in Tel Aviv in 1965.

The *Personal Diary* which Moshe Sharett wrote from October 1953 to November 1956 covers the last years of his political activity as Israel's first foreign minister, including the two years in which he replaced Ben Gurion as the prime minister. It then extends over the first fifteen months of the tormented inactivity following his political demise. Moshe Sharett stopped writing his diary in the middle of a phrase on November 28, 1957. His last notes identify one of his previous collaborators, considered a close personal and political friend, as one of the conspirators against him.

The *Diary*, a 2,400 page document in eight volumes, contains the daily notes and *aide-memoires* in which Sharett recorded current events: personal, family, and party happenings, as well as national and international meetings of prime importance, conversations with his wife or other members of the family alongside administrative questions regarding his ministry and comments on cabinet meetings. The intimate nature of the *Diary*, together with the exceptionally authoritative position of its author, constitutes a rare guarantee of credibility. Unlike other memoirs which have come out of Israel in recent years, and which were written for publication, Sharett's *Diary* hardly can be suspected of distortion, self-glorification or subjectively polemic intentions. It is not surprising at all, therefore, that Sharett's son and his family were subjected to immense pressures to refrain from publication, or at least to submit the document to Labor Party censorship. Sharett's son Ya'acov finally decided to publish the complete writings.

2

Ben Gurion Goes to Sdeh Boker:
Spiritual Retreat as a Tactic _____

Moshe Sharett jotted the first of the daily notes in his personal diary on
October 9, 1953. Shortly before that, Ben Gurion, who was prime minister
and minister of defense, announced his intention to withdraw from
government activities. Sharett, who had been second in command to Ben
Gurion since the pre-state days, was slated to replace him as Israel's prime
minister. He would also retain the foreign ministry.

To public opinion at large, Ben Gurion's intention to retire was
presented grandly as a spiritual exercise, a measure capable of galvanizing
Israeli and Jewish youth and necessary for leading the Zionist sheep back
to the abandoned ideals of pioneering and settlement. In reality, while the
state was spending millions of pounds on the construction of a "hut" for
Ben Gurion in the kibbutz Sdeh Boker in Negev, and on related security
and communications arrangements, the Old Man already knew, and
informed his collaborators, that his absence from the government would
last for two years. Behind the campaign idealizing his withdrawal was a
scenario meticulously prepared by him and his men. Even then, just four
years after the 1948-49 war, the security establishment was ready with
plans for Israel's territorial expansion. The armistice lines established in
Rhodes, although traced so as to grant Israel over a third more than the
territory allotted it by the UN partition resolution in 1947, were considered
unsatisfactory by the army, which aspired to recover *at least* the
boundaries of mandate Palestine. Ben Gurion had theorized already about
the necessity for Israel to become *the* regional power in the Middle East.
Toward the realization of this goal a strategy for the destabilization of the
region also had been drawn: operatively, as we shall see, its pivot for the
next quarter of a century was to be the political-military policy known
under the false name of *"retaliation."* The international conditions for the
implementation of this strategic design, though, had yet to be prepared.

Economic and military aid from the West, in particular, was an essential
condition. At the same time, rapprochement between the West and the
Arab world had to be prevented. Toward this aim, the West had to be
persuaded that Israel would be its best bet in the region militarily, and this
was another of the major objectives of the massive reprisal attacks
launched across the borders by the Israeli army. At the same time, though,
the West should not be alarmed *prematurely* about Israel's intentions,
because it was not ready yet to support these Israeli aims. Ben Gurion's

formal withdrawal, and his (formal) replacement by the "moderate" Sharett, was interpreted by international diplomacy as a sign that Israel was not headed for war. Since the launching of the reprisal actions, such a fear was prevalent in the Arab world.

In the short range, the Israeli design was aimed at slowing down the negotiations between Arab states which were pressing to be armed, and the West, which was reluctant to arm them. In the meantime, the idea that the military actions were intended for no purpose other than their declared one—protecting Israel's civilian populations against guerrilla-type attacks from Arab territories—would gain in credibility under the premiership of Sharett, a man notoriously devoted to moderation and diplomacy. The myth of Israel's security, aimed at generating a consensus, would have its strength enhanced to a greater extent in Ben Gurion's absence. Thus, he went off to Sdeh Boker, accompanied by the aura of a pioneer-saint, and Sharett prepared to take over, or so he thought. In fact, Ben Gurion was to keep control of the real channels of command.

3

Retaliation for War _____

On October 11th, 1953, the foreign minister and would-be premier noted in his diary that he had been to see Ben Zvi, the president of the state:

> Ben Zvi raised as usual some inspired questions . . . such as do we have a chance to occupy the Sinai and how wonderful it would be if the Egyptians started an offensive which we could defeat and follow with an invasion of that desert. He was very disappointed when I told him that the Egyptians show no tendency to facilitate us in this occupation task through a provocative challenge on their side. (11 October 1953, 27)

The next day Ben Gurion informed Sharett that Pinhas Lavon, a staunch supporter of the retaliation policy, would succeed him as the minister of defense, and that he was about to nominate Moshe Dayan as the armed forces chief of staff.

> I said immediately that Moshe Dayan is a soldier only at war time but during peace time he is a politician. The nomination means "politicization" of the headquarters. The new Chief of Staff's immense capacity for plotting and intrigue-making will yield many complications. Ben Gurion admitted to the truth of these definitions and even added that Dayan himself defined himself this way and sought to disqualify himself for the job, but never mind, it will be all right. I left with a sinking heart. (ibid., 29)

Sharett considered the international climate at that time to be unfavorable to Israel: the U.S. has just decided to supply arms to Syria and Iraq, and to arm Egypt soon after the signature of the Canal Zone Agreement. In addition, Israel's constant violations of the UN demands that it cease diversion of the Jordan River and adhere to the Johnston Plan were causing increasing consternation in Western capitals. The West had cultivated the hope that an Arab-Israeli agreement on the diversion of the Jordan waters would, if reached and implemented, become the corner-stone for a wider agreement that would take the wind out of growing anti-Western nationalist tensions in the area.[2] According to the UN observers' chief, Danish General Wagen Benike, "the Israelis have worked and are still working on Arab lands. We [the Israelis] are changing the terrain strategically." (15 October 1955, 39) This, Sharett comments, is really a shameful deed. I enquired several times, and each time I was solemnly assured that no Arab land has been touched. After Benike told me . . . that it was proved to him that our work was begun on Arab land . . . I again interrogated Amir [head of the Water Works Dept.] who now admits the facts. . . . Thus I have been made to appear as a liar in front of the whole world! (31 October 1955, 32)

Fearing that an overdose of Israeli violence at this moment might precipitate a crisis with the West, Sharett tried to block the Kibya reprisal operation which had been endorsed by Ben Gurion on the eve of his departure for a vacation preceding his formal retreat. He pointed out that the minor border incident, which was to have served as a pretext for the planned attack on the West Bank village, had just been publicly condemned by Jordan, and that the Jordanian representatives in the mixed armistice commission had promised to see to it that similar incidents would not be repeated.

I told Lavon that this [attack] will be a grave error, and recalled, citing various precedents, that it was never proved that reprisal actions serve their declared purpose. Lavon smiled . . . and kept to his own idea. . . . Ben Gurion, he said, didn't share my view. (14 October 1953, 37)

According to the first news from the other side, thirty houses have been demolished in one village. This reprisal is unprecedented in its dimensions and in the offensive power used. I walked up and down in my room, helpless and utterly depressed by my feeling of impotence. . . . I was simply horrified by the description in Radio Ramallah's broadcast of the destruction of the Arab village. Tens of houses have been razed to the soil and tens of people killed. I can imagine the storm that will break out tomorrow in the Arab and Western capitals. (15 October 1953, 39)

I must underline that when I opposed the action I didn't even remotely suspect such a bloodbath. I thought that I was opposing one of those actions which have become a routine in the past. Had I even remotely suspected that such a massacre was to be held, I would have raised real hell. (16 October 1953, 44)

Now the army wants to know how we [the foreign ministry] are going to explain the issue. In a joint meeting of army and foreign ministry officials Shmuel Bendor suggested that we say that the army had no part in the operation, but that the inhabitants of the border villages, infuriated by previous incidents and seeking revenge, operated on their own. Such a version will make us appear ridiculous: any child would say that this was a military operation. (16 October 1953)

Yehoshafat Harkabi [then Assistant Chief of Military Intelligence] reported movements of Jordanian troops from Transjordan to the West Bank in two directions . . . from Irbid to the Nablus region and from Amman to Jerusalem. I thought that these movements did not indicate preparations for attack but [were] only preparations for aggression on our side. It is impossible that they did not get the impression that the bombing of Kibya means, if not a calculated plan to cause war, then at least willingness to have one starting as a consequence of the action. "Fati" said that according to Radio Ramallah 56 bodies have already been extracted from the ruins. (17 October 1955, 44–45)

At 3 P.M. Russel [U.S. Charge d'Affaires] and Milton Fried [U.S. Attache] came in . . . Russel's face was gloomy. Kibya was "in the air" . . . I said I will not say a word to justify the attack on Kibya but I must warn against detaching this action from a chain of events and I blamed the uncontrolled situation on the helplessness or the lack of goodwill on the part of Jordan. From that point onwards I attacked U.S. policy as one of the factors which contributed to the encouragement of the Arabs and the isolation of Israel. . . . I have condemned the folly of the [U.S.] idea that we want war and all our actions in the South and in the North are directed exclusively to bring it about. . . . Russel asked . . . if we shall disavow Kibya. I said that I cannot answer. . . . Katriel ("Salmon") [Israel's military attache in London] came up with the idea of a "diversion": the Kibya affair would attract all the attention unless we are able to invent some other dramatic issue. (17 October 1953, 45)

[In the cabinet meeting] I condemned the Kibya affair that exposed us in front of the whole world as a gang of blood-suckers, capable of mass massacres regardless, it seems, of whether their actions may lead to war. I warned that this stain will stick to us and will not be washed away for many years to come. . . . It was decided that a communique on Kibya will be published and Ben Gurion [back from his vacation for the occasion] was to write it. I insisted on including an expression of regret. Ben Gurion insisted on excluding any responsibility of the army*: the civilian citizens of the border areas, enraged by the constant murders, have taken justice into their hands. After all [he said] the border settlements are full of arms and the settlers are ex-soldiers. . . . I said that no one in the world will believe such a story and we shall only expose ourselves as liars. But I couldn't seriously demand that the communique explicitly affirm the army's responsibility because this would have made it impossible to condemn the act and we will have ended up approving this monstrous bloodbath.[3] (18 October 1953, 51)

For Sharett as well, the army was irreproachable. But then why blame the army when the decision had been taken on a political level? Beyond this, however, emerges a significant detail. Clearly, *the security of the Israeli border population could hardly be more jeopardized than by attributing to them the responsibility for a bloodbath such as Kibya's.* Encouraging an escalation of acts of revenge and further reprisals clearly had a cynical provocative intent, as did Lavon's smile when Sharett tried to convince him of the fatuousness of the relations in relation to their *declared purpose.* From the beginning, in fact, the retaliation policy was headed elsewhere: the stronger the tensions in the region, the more demoralized the Arab populations and destabilized the Arab regimes, the

*See Appendix 1.

stronger the pressures for the transfer of the concentrations of Palestinian refugees from places near the border away into the interior of the Arab world—and the better it was for the preparation of the next war. In the meantime, the army could be kept in training. On October 19 a cabinet meeting was convened where:

> Ben Gurion spoke for two and a half hours on the army's preparations for the second round . . . [He] presented detailed figures on the growth of the military force of the Arab countries which (he said) will reach its peak in 1956. (19 October 1953, 54)

It was not a prophecy. This meant that Israel would wage war within that date. Sharett added:

> As I listened . . . I was thinking . . . that we should proceed against the danger with non-military means: propose daring and concrete solutions for the Refugee problem through the payment of compensations, improve our relations with the powers, search ceaselessly for an understanding with Egypt.

This was certainly *not* what the Israeli security establishment was driving at. On October 26, 1953, a group of American Zionist leaders was lectured to, in Israel, by Colonel Matti Peled. The conclusions from that presentation, Sharett noted, were "implicitly clear":

> One, that the army considers the present border with Jordan as absolutely unacceptable. Two, that the army is planning war in order to occupy the rest of Western Eretz Israel.[4] (26 October 1953, 81)

Although formulated in very mild terms, the Security Council condemnation of Israel for the Kibya attack pushed Sharett to impose an embargo on reprisal actions unless he personally authorized them. For a while, no spectacular actions were undertaken, but minor, unauthorized Israeli incursions into the West Bank and Gaza continued to make civilian victims. The murder of a Jordanian doctor on the Bethlehem-Hebron road, which was reported by the press, raised the premier's suspicions, for example. Enraged, he learned that this, in fact, was Israeli work. This, and other similar investigations, were to fray the relations between the military and the prime minister. In January 1954, Dayan requested and obtained a meeting with all Mapai's ministers:

> Moshe Dayan brought out one plan after the other for "direct action." The first—what should be done to force open the blockade in the straits of Eilat. A ship flying the Israeli flag should be sent, and if the Egyptians will bomb it we

should bomb the Egyptian base from the air, or [we should] conquer Ras-e-Naqueb or open our way from the south to the Gaza Strip up to the coast. There was a general uproar. I asked him, Do you realize this would mean war with Egypt? He said, of course. (31 January 1954, 331)

War with Egypt was to remain a major ambition of Israel's security establishment, but the time was not yet ripe. On February 25, Ben Gurion, himself put the brakes on his collaborators' impatience when he rejected Lavon's proposal "to go ahead immediately with the plan for the separation of the Gaza Strip from Egypt." The Old Man was determined to stick to *his* timetable. Now, Sharett noted later, "Ben Gurion suggested to concentrate on action against Syria." (27 February 1954, 377)

4

A Historical Opportunity to
Occupy Southern Syria _____

At the above cited meeting on January 31, 1954 Moshe Dayan went on to outline his war plans. Sharett's note for that day continues:

> The second plan—action against the interference of the Syrians with our fishing in the Lake of Tiberias. . . . The third—if, due to internal problems in Syria, Iraq invades that country . . . we should advance [militarily, into Syria] and realize a series of "faits accomplis." . . . The interesting conclusion to be drawn from all this regards the direction in which the new Chief of Staff is thinking. I am extremely worried. (31 January 1954, 332)

On February 25, 1954, Syrian troops stationed in Aleppo revolted against Adib Shishakly's regime.

> After lunch Lavon took me aside and started trying to persuade me: This is the right moment to act—this is the time to move forward and occupy the Syrian border positions beyond the Demilitarized Zone. Syria is disintegrating. A State with whom we signed an armistice agreement exists no more. Its government is about to fall and there is no other power in view. Moreover, Iraq has practically moved into Syria. This is an historical opportunity, we shouldn't miss it.

> I was reluctant to approve such a blitz-plan and saw ourselves on the verge of an abyss of disastrous adventure. I asked if he suggests to act immediately and I was shocked when I realized that he does. I said that if indeed Iraq will move into Syria with its army it will be a revolutionary turn which will . . . justify far reaching conclusions, but for the time being this is only a danger, not a fact. It is not even clear if Shishakly will fall: he may survive. We ought to wait before making any decision. He repeated that time was precious and we must act so as not to miss an opportunity which otherwise might be lost forever. Again I answered that under the circumstances right now I cannot approve any such action. Finally I said that next Saturday we would be meeting with Ben Gurion . . .and we could consult him then on the matter. I saw that he was extremely displeased by the delay. However, he had no choice but to agree. (25 February 1954, 374)

The next day the Shishakly regime actually fell. The following day, February 27, Sharett was present at a meeting where Lavon and Dayan reported to Ben Gurion that what happened in Syria was "a typical Iraqi action." The two proposed again that the Israeli army be put on the march. Ben Gurion, "electrified," agreed. Sharett reiterated his opposition, pointing to the certainty of a Security Council condemnation, the possibility of the use against Israel of the Tripartite Declaration of 1950, hence the probability of a "shameful failure." The three objected that "our entrance [into Syria] is justified in view of the situation in Syria. This is an act of defense of our border area." Sharett closed the discussion by insisting on the need for further discussion in the cabinet meeting, scheduled for the next morning:

> Lavon's face wore a depressed expression. He understood this to be the end of the matter. (27 February 1954, 377)

On Sunday, February 28, the press reported that no Iraqi troops had entered Syria. The situation in Damascus was under the complete control of President Hashem Al Atassi. The cabinet approved Sharett's position and rejected Lavon's vehement appeal not to miss a historical opportunity. Lavon said "the U.S. is about to betray us and ally itself with the Arab world." We should "demonstrate our strength and indicate to the U.S. that our life depends on this so that they will not dare do anything against us." The premier's victory, however, was to be short-lived.

Until that time the Syrian-Israeli border presented no particular problems to the Israelis. When tensions developed, it was almost invariably due to Israeli provocations, such as the irrigation work on lands belonging to Arab farmers, which was condemned by the UN; or the use of military patrol boats against Syrian fishermen fishing in the Lake of Tiberias. No Syrian regime could afford to refrain from offering some minimum protection to its border citizens against Israeli attacks or the taking away of their livelihoods, but neither did the rulers of Damascus feel stable enough to wish to be dragged into a major conflict with their southern neighbor. Clashes were therefore minor, and essentially seasonal. No security arguments could be credibly invoked to justify an expansionist program, or any other aggression against Syria.

On December 12, 1954, however, a Syrian civilian plane was hijacked by Israeli war planes shortly after its takeoff, and forced to land at Lydda airport. Passengers and crew were detained and interrogated for two days, until stormy international protests forced the Israelis to release them. Furious, Sharett wrote to Lavon on December 22:

> It must be clear to you that we had no justification whatsoever to seize the plane, and that once forced down we should have immediately released it and not held the passengers under interrogation for 48 hours. I have no reason to doubt the truth of the factual affirmation of the U.S. State Department that our action was without precedent in the history of international practice.

. . . What shocks and worries me is the narrow-mindedness and the short-sightedness of our military leaders. They seem to presume that the State of Israel may—or even must—behave in the realm of international relations according to the laws of the jungle. (22 December 1954, 607)

Sharett also protested to Lavon against the scandalous press campaign, which he suspected was inspired by the security establishment and which was aimed at convincing public opinion

that the Syrian plane was stopped and forced down because it violated Israeli sovereignty and perhaps endangered its security. As a result, the public does not understand why such a plane was released and naturally it concludes that we have here an unjustified concession on the part of the government. (ibid.)

On December 11, the day before Israel set this world precedent for air piracy, five Israeli soldiers were captured inside Syrian territory while mounting wiretapping installations on the Syrian telephone network. A month later, on January 13, 1955, one of them committed suicide in prison. The official Israeli version is, once again, that the five had been abducted in Israeli territory, taken to Syria, and tortured. The result was a violent emotional upsurge in Israel, all the more so as this news arrived shortly after the condemnation in Cairo of members of an Israeli terrorist ring which had been described to public opinion as an anti-Jewish frame-up. The prime minister confided to his personal diary:

A young boy has been sacrificed for nothing. . . . Now they will say that his blood is on my hands. If I hadn't ordered the release of the Syrian plane [we would have had our hostages and] the Syrians could have been forced to free the five. The boy . . . would have been alive . . . our soldiers have not been kidnapped in Israeli territory by Syrian invaders as the army spokesman announced . . . . They penetrated into Syria and not accidentally but in order to take care of a wiretapping installation, connected to a Syrian telephone line . . . the young men were sent without any experienced person, they were not instructed what to do in case of failure and the result was that in the first interrogation they broke down and told the whole truth. . . . I have no doubt that the press and the Knesset will cry about torture. On the other hand, it is possible that the boy committed suicide because he broke down during the interrogation and only later he understood what a disaster he has brought upon his comrades and what he did to the state. Possibly his comrades tormented him afterwards. Anyway, his conscience probably caused him to take this terrible step. (3 January 1955, 649)

Isser [Harel, then Shin Bet chief] warned me of what may happen to me personally as a result of the suicide. A poisonous attack is being organized against me. . . . It is particularly necessary to take care of what is happening in the army and to prevent lawless riots. (14 January 1955, 653)

It is clear that Dayan's intention . . . is to get [Syrian] hostages in order to obtain the release of our prisoners in Damascus. He put it into his head that it is necessary to take hostages, and would not let go. (10 February 1955, 714)

Nineteen years later, Dayan, then minister of defense in Golda Meir's government, ordered his troops to move into a school, regardless of the danger to Israeli civilians including children, in Ma'alot, with the sole aim of preventing Palestinian guerrillas from obtaining, through the taking of hostages, the release of their Palestinian comrades jailed and tortured under the military occupation of the West Bank and Gaza. On that, as on other similar occasions, a virulent and poisonous Zionist campaign, widely echoed in the Western media, declared the Palestinian liberation movement's attempt to free prisoners by taking hostages as intolerable, barbaric, savage, murderous, and terrorist. When did these same media call Moshe Dayan a *terrorist*?

Israeli plots against Syria in the fifties were not only limited to expansionist and terrorist projects. On July 31, 1955, a senior foreign ministry aide, Gideon Raphael, reported to Sharett on a couple of "interesting meetings" he had held with Arab exiles in Europe. One of these was with ex-Syrian Premier Hosni Barazi:

Hosni wants to get back in power, and is ready to accept help from anyone: from Turkey, in exchange for Syria's future entrance into the Ankara-Baghdad pact; from the U.S., in exchange for Syria's future alliance with the West; with Israel, in exchange for a peace agreement. (31 July 1955, 1099)

Peace, however, was the last thing Israel was interested in. Israel's support would require another price:

Meanwhile he says to us give-give: money for newspapers, money to buy off personalities, money to buy off political parties. Gideon [suggested to him that] . . . he himself is a big land owner, and why won't he get together a group of land owners, initiate a big plan of settling refugees. . . . Hosni listened, said it was a wonderful idea . . . but only after he regains power, and until he regains power he needs a payment in advance. (31 July 1955, 1100)

A year later, a week before his final fall from the government, Sharett got a last report on Israel's subversive activities in Syria from his advisor on Arab affairs, "Josh" Palmon:

Our contacts with [Adib] Shishakly [the exiled Syrian dictator overthrown in 1954] have been strengthened. The guidelines for common action after his return to power (if he returns!) have been established. We have decided on guidelines to contact the U.S. in regard to this issue. (12 June 1956, 1430)

None of these "historical opportunities" regarding Syria actually materialized at that time, nor, however, did Israel ever abandon its plans to install a puppet regime in Damascus. But in Lebanon as well, the precise operational blueprints elaborated in *1954* waited two decades before being put into action.[5]

5

Let Us Create
A Maronite State in Lebanon _____

The February 27, 1954 meeting among Ben Gurion, Sharett, Lavon and Dayan has already been mentioned in connection with Israel's invasion plans of Egypt and Syria. In that same meeting a concrete proposal was outlined to disrupt Israel's most peaceful neighbor at that time, Lebanon. In this case, Israel's hegemonic ambitions did not even *pretend* to wear the phony fig leaf of security or defense.

> Then he [Ben Gurion] passed on to another issue. This is the time, he said, to push Lebanon, that is, the Maronites in that country, to proclaim a Christian State. I said that this was nonsense. The Maronites are divided. The partisans of Christian separatism are weak and will dare do nothing. A Christian Lebanon would mean their giving up Tyre, Tripoli, the Beka'a. There is no force that could bring Lebanon back to its pre-World War I dimensions, and all the more so because in that case it would lose its economic raison-d'etre. Ben Gurion reacted furiously. He began to enumerate the historical justification for a restricted Christian Lebanon. If such a development were to take place, the Christian Powers would not dare oppose it. I claimed that there was no factor ready to create such a situation, and that if we were to push and encourage it on our own we would get ourselves into an adventure that will place shame on us. Here came a wave of insults regarding my lack of daring and my narrow-mindedness. We ought to send envoys and spend money. I said there was no money. The answer was that there is no such thing. The money must be found, if not in the Treasury then at the Jewish Agency! For such a project it is worthwhile throwing away one hundred thousand, half a million, a million dollars. When this happens a decisive change will take place in the Middle East, a new era will start. I got tired of struggling against a whirlwind. (27 February 1954, 377)

The next day Ben Gurion sent Sharett the following letter:

To Moshe Sharett   Sdeh Boker
The Prime Minister   February 27, 1954

> Upon my withdrawal from the government I decided in my heart to desist from intervening and expressing my opinion on current political affairs so as not to make things difficult for the government in any way. And if you hadn't called on me, the three of you, yourself, Lavon and Dayan, I would not have, of my own

accord, expressed an opinion on what is being done or what ought to be done. But as you called me, I deem it my duty to comply with your wishes, and especially with your own wish as Prime Minister. Therefore, I permit myself to go back to one issue which you did not approve of and discuss it again, and this is the issue of Lebanon.

. . . It is clear that Lebanon is the weakest link in the Arab League. The other minorities in the Arab States are all Muslim, except for the Copts. But Egypt is the most compact and solid of the Arab States and the majority there consists of one solid block, of one race, religion and language, and the Christian minority does not seriously affect their political and national unity. Not so the Christians in Lebanon. They are a majority in the historical Lebanon and this majority has a tradition and a culture different from those of the other components of the League. Also within the wider borders (this was the worst mistake made by France when it extended the borders of Lebanon), the Muslims are not free to do as they wish, even if they are a majority there (and I don't know if they are, indeed, a majority) for fear of the Christians. The creation of a Christian State is therefore a natural act; it has historical roots and it will find support in wide circles in the Christian world, both Catholic and Protestant. In normal times this would be almost impossible. First and foremost because of the lack of initiative and courage of the Christians. But at times of confusion, or revolution or civil war, things take on another aspect, and even the weak declares himself to be a hero. Perhaps (there is never any certainty in politics) now is the time to bring about the creation of a Christian State in our neighborhood. Without our initiative and our vigorous aid this will not be done. It seems to me that this is the *central duty,* or at least one of the central duties, of our foreign policy. This means that time, energy and means ought to be invested in it and that we must act in all possible ways to bring about a radical change in Lebanon. Sasson . . . and our other Arabists must be mobilized. If money is necessary, no amount of dollars should be spared, although the money may be spent in vain. We must concentrate all our efforts on this issue. . . . This is a historical opportunity. Missing it will be unpardonable. There is no challenge against the World Powers in this. . . . Everything should be done, in my opinion, rapidly and at full steam.

The goal will not be reached of course, without a restriction of Lebanon's borders. But if we can find men in Lebanon and exiles from it who will be ready to mobilize for the creation of a Maronite state, extended borders and a large Muslim population will be of no use to them and this will not constitute a disturbing factor.

I don't know if we have people in Lebanon—but there are various ways in which the proposed experiment can be carried out.

D.B.G
(27 February 1954, 2397-2398)

Sharett responded a few weeks later:

Mr. David Ben Gurion   March 18, 1954
Sdeh Boker.

. . . A permanent assumption of mine is that if sometimes there is some reason to interfere from the outside in the internal affairs of some country in order to support a political movement inside it aiming toward some target it is only when that movement shows some independent activity which there is a chance to enhance and maybe to bring to success by encouragement and help from the outside. There is no point in trying to create from the outside a movement that does not exist at all inside . . . it is impossible to inject life into a dead body.

As far as I know, in Lebanon today exists no movement aiming at transforming the country into a Christian State governed by the Maronite community. . . .

This is not surprising. The transformation of Lebanon into a Christian State as a result of an outside initiative is unfeasible today . . . I don't exclude the possibility of accomplishing this goal in the wake of a wave of shocks that will sweep the Middle East . . . will destroy the present constellations and will form others. But in the present Lebanon, with its present territorial and demographic dimensions and its international relations, no serious initiative of the kind is imaginable.

The Christians do not constitute the majority in Lebanon. Nor are they a unified block, politically speaking or community-wise. The Orthodox minority in Lebanon tends to identify with their brethren in Syria. They will not be ready to go to war for a Christian Lebanon, that is for a Lebanon smaller than it is today, and detached from the Arab League. On the contrary, they would probably not be opposed to a Lebanon united to Syria, as this would contribute to strengthening their own community and the Orthodox community throughout the region. . . . In fact, there are more Orthodox Christians in Syria than in Lebanon, and the Orthodox in Syria and Lebanon together are more numerous than the Maronites.

As to the Maronites, the great majority among them has for years now supported those pragmatic political leaders of their community who have long since abandoned the dream of a Christian Lebanon, and put all their cards on a Christian-Muslim coalition in that country. These leaders have developed the consciousness that there is no chance for an isolated Maronite Lebanon and that the historical perspective of their community means a partnership with the Muslims in power, and in a membership of Lebanon in the League, hoping and believing that these factors can guarantee that the Lebanese Muslims will abandon their longings for a unification of Lebanon with Syria and will enhance the development among them of a feeling for Lebanese independence.

Therefore, the great majority of the Maronite community is liable to see in any attempt at raising the flag of territorial shrinking and Maronite power a dangerous attempt at subverting the status of their community, its security and even its very existence. Such an initiative would seem disastrous to them because it could tear apart the pattern of Christian-Muslim collaboration in the present Lebanon which was created through great efforts and sacrifices for an entire generation; because it would mean throwing the Lebanese Muslims into the Syrian embrace; and finally, because it would fatally bring about the historical disaster of an annexation of Lebanon to Syria and the annihilation of the former's personality through its dilution in a big Muslim state.

You may object that these arguments are irrelevant as the Plan is based on tearing away from Lebanon the Muslim provinces of Tyre, the Beka'a and Tripoli. But who can predict that these provinces will actually give up their ties to Lebanon and their political and economic connection to Beirut? Who can assure that the Arab League will be ready to give up the status that Lebanon's affiliation confers to it . . .? Who will vouch that the bloody war that will inevitably explode as a result of such an attempt will be limited to Lebanon and not drag Syria into the battlefield immediately? Who can be sure that the Western Powers will look on as observers and will not intervene in the experiment before a Christian Lebanon will have been realized? Who can guarantee that the Maronite leadership itself will not become aware of all the above considerations and will therefore back out of such a dangerous adventure?

. . . There are also decisive economic arguments against it. We are not discussing the issue in 1920/21 . . . but 30 years later. Mount Lebanon has meanwhile integrated into one organic unit with the coastal plane of Tyre and Sidon, the Valley of Baalbeck and the city of Tripoli. They are commercially and economically interdependent and inseparable. Mount Lebanon was not a self-sufficient unit even before World War I. . . . The annexation of the three regions plus the city of Beirut to the Lebanese State has rendered possible the creation of a balanced economy. A return to the past would not just mean a surgical operation but also a disintegration leading to the end of Lebanon. . . .

I cannot imagine, even from this viewpoint alone, that any serious organization would collaborate with a plan that in my opinion would entail Lebanon's economic suicide.

When all this has been said, [I should add that] I would not have objected, and on the contrary I would have certainly been favorable to the idea, of actively aiding any manifestation of agitation in the Maronite community tending to strengthen its isolationist tendencies, even if there were no real chances of achieving the goals; I would have considered positive the very existence of such an agitation and the destabilization it could bring about, the trouble it would have caused the League, the diversion of attention from the Arab-Israeli complications that it would have caused, and the very kindling of a fire made up of impulses toward Christian independence. But what can I do when such an agitation is nonexistent? . . . In the present condition, I am afraid that any attempt on our part would be considered as lightheadedness and superficiality or worse—as an adventurous speculation upon the well being and existence of others and a readiness to sacrifice their basic good for the benefit of a temporary tactical advantage for Israel.

Moreover, if this plan is not kept a secret but becomes known—a danger which cannot be underestimated in the Middle Eastern circumstances—the damage which we shall suffer . . . would not be compensated even by an eventual success of the operation itself. . . .

M.S.
(18 March 1954, 2398–2400)

On April 24 a fleeting note in the *Diary* informs us that "contacts with certain circles in Lebanon" had been discussed that day between the premier and some of his collaborators in the foreign ministry. The next time Lebanon is mentioned is on February 12, 1955: Neguib Sfeir, "an adventurer and a visionary" whom Sharett had known since 1920, had just paid a visit to the Israeli ambassador in Rome, Eliahu Sasson,

> apparently on behalf of Lebanon's President Camille Chamoun. Lebanon would be ready to sign a separate peace if we accept the following three conditions: (a) guarantee Lebanon's borders; (b) come to Lebanon's aid if it is attacked by Syria; (c) buy Lebanon's agricultural surplus. Sasson ... suggested a meeting between himself and Chamoun during the latter's next visit to Rome. (12 February 1955, 723)

On May 16, during a joint meeting of senior officials of the defense and foreign affairs ministries, Ben Gurion again raised the demand that Israel do something about Lebanon. The moment was particularly propitious, he maintained, due to renewed tensions between Syria and Iraq, and internal trouble in Syria. Dayan immediately expressed his enthusiastic support:

> According to him [Dayan] the only thing that's necessary is to find an officer, even just a Major. We should either win his heart or buy him with money, to make him agree to declare himself the savior of the Maronite population. Then the Israeli army will enter Lebanon, will occupy the necessary territory, and will create a Christian regime which will ally itself with Israel. The territory from the Litani southward will be totally annexed to Israel and everything will be all right. If we were to accept the advice of the Chief of Staff we would do it tomorrow, without awaiting a signal from Baghdad.
>
> ...I did not want to bicker with Ben Gurion...in front of his officers and limited myself to saying that this might mean...war between Israel and Syria.... At the same time I agreed to set up a joint commission composed of officials of the Foreign Affairs Ministry and the army to deal with Lebanese affairs. .... [According to Ben Gurion] this commission should relate to the Prime Minister. (16 May 1954, 966)
>
> The Chief of Staff supports a plan to hire a [Lebanese] officer who will agree to serve as a puppet so that the Israeli army may appear as responding to his appeal "to liberate Lebanon from its Muslim oppressors." This will of course be a crazy adventure.... We must try to prevent dangerous complications. The commission must be charged with research tasks and prudent actions directed at encouraging Maronite circles who reject Muslim pressures and agree to lean on us. (28 May 1954, 1024)

The "prudent actions" continued. On September 22, a mysterious incident occurred. A bus was attacked in Galilee, near Safad. Two persons were killed and ten wounded. Even before an investigation could establish where the aggressors came from (and there were, at that moment, three contradictory hypotheses), Dayan demanded a reprisal action against Lebanon. A Lebanese village suspected to be the attackers' base had already been chosen. Its population would be evacuated in the night, its houses blown up. Sharett objected to Israel's opening a new front along a border which had been totally peaceful since 1948. But this was exactly what Dayan sought: the destabilization of Lebanon and the search for a forerunner to Major Sa'd Haddad who declared a Maronite state in 1979. The fulfillment of his disruptive plans would have found an ideal point of departure in this terrorist action.

Sharett, however, vetoed an immediate action. At this point the Israeli plot against Lebanon was suspended for other reasons. On October 1, 1955, the U.S. government, through the CIA, gave Israel the "green light" to attack Egypt. The energies of Israel's security establishment became wholly absorbed by the preparations for the war which would take place exactly one year later. In the summer of 1956, in preparation for the Sinai-Suez operation, the close military and political alliance with France was clinched. It would last practically until the eve of the 1967 war, and would prevent Israel, especially following De Gaulle's rise to power in France in 1957, from implementing its plans for the dismemberment of a country Paris considered as belonging to the French sphere of influence. Israeli bombings of South Lebanon, specifically intended to destabilize that country, were to start in 1968—after the 1967 war, after Dayan's nomination as defense minister in Levi Eshkol's cabinet, and after Israel's definite transition from the alliance with France to that with the United States.[6] From that moment on, this unholy alliance was to use every possible means constantly to escalate terrorist violence and political subversion in Lebanon, according to Israel's blueprints of the fifties. All this, it is hardly necessary to recall, was hatched when no Palestinian guerrillas were remotely in view.[7] If anything, the difficulties Israel encountered throughout all these years in consummating its long-standing ambition to divide Lebanon and separate it from the Arab world constitute one more proof of the external and alien nature of these plots in respect to the authentic aspirations of the Lebanese people regardless of their religious faith.

6

Sacred Terrorism _____

On March 17, 1954, a bus traveling from Eilat to Beersheba was attacked in Ma'aleh Ha'akrabim crossroads. Ten passengers were killed and four survived. According to Israeli army trackers, all traces of the perpetrators disappeared at a distance of ten kilometers from the Jordanian border, inside Israeli territory, due to the rocky nature of the terrain. One of the survivors, a sergeant responsible for security arrangements on the trip, testified that the attackers were "Beduin." Another survivor, a woman, said they were "five men wearing long robes." The army, according to Sharett, "then dispatched some of its Arab informers to the village of Tel Tsafi, [on the Jordanian side of the border] opposite Sodom." Upon their return, the informers reported that "a group of 8-10 persons had been seen crossing the borders westward [that day]" by Tel Tsafi villagers. Quite apart from the fact that it was customary, since time immemorial, for the area's nomad population to cross back and forth at that point, there must have been something much too strange about this story of informers and villagers offering evidence. Colonel Hutcheson, the American chairman of the mixed Jordanian-Israeli Armistice Commission, did not take it seriously. Summing up the Commission's inquiry, Colonel Hutcheson in fact officially announced that "from the testimonies of the survivors it is not proved that all the murderers were Arabs." (23 March 1954, 411)

Moreover, in a confidential report dated March 24, and addressed to General Benike, Hutcheson explicitly attributed the attack on the bus to terrorists intent on heightening the tensions in the area as well as on creating trouble for the present government.[8] Thereupon the Israelis left the Armistice Commission in protest, and launched a worldwide campaign against "Arab terrorism" and "bloodthirsty hatred" of Jews. From his retreat in Sdeh Boker, Ben Gurion demanded that Israel occupy Jordanian territory and threatened to leave the Mapai party leadership if Sharett's policy were once again to have the upper hand. Lavon, too, pressed for action. On April 4, the premier wrote to Ben Gurion:

> I heard that after Ma'aleh Ha'akrabim you thought that we should occupy Jordanian territory. In my opinion such a step would have dragged us into a war with a Jordan supported by Britain, while the U.S. would have condemned us in

front of the whole world and treated us as an aggressor. For Israel this could have meant disaster and perhaps destruction. (4 April 1954, 453)

Sharett attempted to avert military action. He told officials of the Ministry of Foreign Affairs that "we were all of the opinion that a retaliation for such a bloodshed will only weaken its horrible impression and will put us on the same level as the murderers on the other side. It would be better for us to use the Ma'aleh Ha'akrabim incident as a lever for a political attack on the Powers so that they will exercise unprecedented pressure on Jordan." He also pointed out that a retaliation would weaken the effect of the massive propaganda campaign which, he noted in his diary, should counter "the attention given by the American press to the Jordanian version . . . according to which the Ma'aleh Ha'akrabim massacre was committed by the Israelis." Not only in public but in his private notes, the prime minister declared his reluctance to believe this version.[9]

Deep down in his heart, however, Sharett too must have had his unconfessed doubts. He not only blocked the proposed military actions, but decided that Israel should refrain from complaining to the Security Council, i.e., from an international debate which he thought might be counterproductive. He felt he had acted wisely when Dayan, in the course of a conversation on April 23, let drop in passing that "he is not convinced that the Ma'aleh Ha'akrabim massacre was the work of an organized military gang." He later learned from the British journalist Jon Kimche that Dayan had said about Ma'aleh Ha'akrabim that "UN reports are often more accurate than ours. . . ." He wrote: "From another source I heard this week that Dayan said to Israeli journalists that it was not proved that the Ma'aleh Ha'akrabim gang was Jordanian—it is possible that it was local."

Of course, it didn't occur to Sharett to open an internal investigation in order to find out the truth. On the contrary, he insisted on the removal of Colonel Hutcheson from his post as a condition for Israel's return to the Armistice Commission. The military, though, were reluctant to give in to his veto on a new attack on the West Bank. Taking for a pretext not Ma'aleh Ha'akrabim but a subsequent minor incident in the Jerusalem corridor area, on the night of March 28 the army launched a massive attack on the village of Nahlin, near Bethlehem. Dozens of civilians were killed and wounded, the houses demolished, the village—another Palestinian village—completely destroyed.

I said [to Teddy Kollek (then senior aide in the Prime Minister's Office, today mayor of Jerusalem)]: here we are, back at the point of departure—are we headed for war or do we want to prevent war? According to Teddy the army leadership is imbued with war appetites. . . .[They are] completely blind to economic problems and to the complexities of international relations. (31 March 1954, 426)

Arab capitals, too, were persuaded that the Israeli escalation of self-provoked incidents, terrorism and renewed retaliation meant that Israel was preparing the ground for war. They, therefore, stationed military reinforcements along the borders and took strong measures to prevent any infiltration into Israel. This in turn worried the Israelis. "The situation along the borders is better than it has been for a long time and actually it is quite satisfactory," Dayan told a journalist friend who reported it to Sharett on May 17. A new and more subtle strategy of covert aggression was thereupon introduced by the Israeli army. Its aim: to bypass both the Arab security arrangements and Sharett's reluctance to authorize attacks across the border. Small patrols slipped into the West Bank and Gaza with precise directives to engage isolated Egyptian or Jordanian military patrols, or to penetrate into villages for sabotage or murder actions. Invariably, each such action was falsely described later by an official announcement as having occurred in Israeli territory. Once attacked, the military spokesman would explain, the patrol proceeded to pursue the aggressors into enemy territory. Almost daily actions of this kind, carried out by Arik Sharon's special paratroops, caused a great number of casualties. Regularly, the prime minister was left to guess how things really went. Between April and June he noted in his diary that he learned by chance, for example, of the coldblooded murder of a young Palestinian boy who happened to find himself in the Israeli patrol's way near his village in the West Bank. With regard to another incident he wrote:

> Finally I have discovered the secret official version on the Tel Tsafi action—two Arabs that we have sent attacked the Mukhtar who was supposedly said to have been involved in a theft, and killed his wife: in another incident a unit of ours crossed the border "by mistake;" in a third incident three of our soldiers were patrolling deep inside Jordanian territory, ran into the National Guard which opened fire (who will check?), returned fire and killed four. (31 May 1954, 523)

> Hundreds of workers in Sodom know the truth and laugh at [the denial of the murder broadcast by] the Israeli radio and the Israeli government.

> This situation endangers the life and the enterprise in Sodom. . . . Is the army allowed to act in that way according to its own whims and endanger such a vital enterprise? (13 May 1954, 514)

On June 27 an Israeli paratrooper unit crossed the border, "by mistake," according to the official communique, 13 kilometers deep into the West Bank, where it attacked and seriously damaged the Jordanian army base of Azun, east of Qalqilia. "Uncivilized, here they go lying again in front of everybody," was Sharett's ingenious comment about the army spokesman's announcement.

What Sharett feared most was Western reaction. A number of U.S. expressions of alarm presented during those weeks to the Israeli government were registered in the premier's diary.

> Reports by U.S. embassies in Arab capitals, studied in Washington, have produced in the State Department the conviction that an Israeli plan of retaliations, to be realized according to a pre-fixed timetable, exists, and that the goal is that of a steady escalation of the tension in the area in order to bring about a war.[10] American diplomacy is also convinced that it is Israel's intention to sabotage the U.S. negotiations with Egypt, and also those with Iraq and Turkey, aimed at the establishment of pro-Western alliances. (14 April 1955)

This analysis was correct. It was reconfirmed in the following weeks by Israel's rejection of border security proposals previously accepted by Egypt, including the creation of mixed Israel-Egypt-UN patrols, and the mining of certain border areas. Such arrangements, Dayan affirmed, "will tie our hands." It would be confirmed further in July, when an Israeli terrorist ring charged with sabotaging Western institutions in Cairo and Alexandria was broken up by the Egyptian authorities.

Israeli border terrorism in its various forms was to continue unperturbed during the next two years, up to the very eve of the Sinai-Suez war, and, of course, beyond. Sharett noted an episode "of the worst type" in March 1955, immediately after the Gaza operation.

> The army informed Tkoa . . . [responsible for Armistice Commission affairs in the Foreign Ministry] that last night a "private" revenge action was carried out following the killing of the young man and woman, Oded Wegmeister and Shoshana Hartsion, who went on a trip on their own around Ein Gedi [in Jordanian territory]. According to the army version a group of young men, including the girl's brother, Meir Hartsion . . . crossed the border, attacked a group of Beduin, and killed five of them. The army says it supposedly knew that such an initiative was being prepared and intended to prevent it, but according to its information the action was scheduled for tonight and the assumption was that there is time for preventive action, but the boys advanced the action and this is the reason that what happened—happened. Today, the Jordanians issued a completely different version: twenty Israeli soldiers committed the murders—they attacked six Beduin, killed five and left one alive and told him that this is an act of revenge for the couple . . . so that he will tell others about it. The army spokesman tonight announced . . . that no army unit was involved in the operation. . . .

> This may be taken as a decisive proof that we have decided to pass on to a general bloody offensive on all fronts: yesterday Gaza, today something on the Jordanian border, tomorrow the Syrian DMZ, and so on. In the Cabinet meeting tomorrow, I will demand that the killers be put on trial as criminals. (5 March 1955, 816)

> Ben Gurion [back in the government as Minister of Defense in the wake of the Lavon Affair] reported to the cabinet . . . how our four youngsters captured the Beduin boys one by one, how they took them to the wadi, how they knifed them

to death one after the other, and how they interrogated each one of them, before killing him, on the identity of the murderers of the boy and the girl and how they could not understand the answers to their questions, since they do not speak Arabic. The group was headed by Meir Hartsion from kibbutz Ein Harod. . . . They gave themselves up to the army and fully admitted what they have done.

Both Ben Gurion and I saw an advantage in trying them in a military court . . . educationally it is desirable that the lengthy imprisonment to which they will be condemned will be given by a military court, since the army will not have any respect for a punishment coming from a civilian court. . . . In the evening the Minister of Justice and the General Prosecutor informed me that there is no legal way to turn them over to a military court. . . . I contacted Ben Gurion and arranged that he will give instructions to the army to turn them over to the police. . . . By the way, Hartsion . . . and his three friends are paratrooper reservists. (6 March 1955, 817)

[While Purim festivities are being celebrated in the streets of Tel Aviv] The radio is broadcasting cheerful music . . . some of which expresses much talent, spiritual grace and longing for original beauty. I meditated on the substance and destiny of this People who is capable of subtle delicacy, of such deep love for people and of such honest aspiration for beauty and nobility, and at the same time cultivates among its best youth youngsters capable of calculated, coldblooded murder, by knifing the bodies of young defenseless Beduin. Which of these two biblical souls will win over the other in this People? (8 March 1955, 823)

Finally the four have been consigned to the police but now they refuse to talk. . . . I phoned Ben Gurion. . . . "It's their legitimate right," he said. . . . [He added] that their confession to the army cannot serve for their incrimination by a civilian court. From a juridical viewpoint this may be so, but from a public point of view this is a scandal. (10 March 1955, 828)

The police chief approached the Chief of Staff and asked if the army is willing to aid the police interrogation. . . . The Chief of Staff said that he will ask the Minister of Defense and then answered in his name that he does not agree to have an interrogation in the army . . . it is clear that the army is covering up for the guys.

Isser [Har'el] senses that almost no one in the country condemns the youngsters who murdered the Beduin. Public opinion is definitely on their side.

When I arrived in Tel Aviv an officer . . . came to tell me that the whole revenge operation was organized with the active help of Arik Sharon, the commander of the paratroopers battalion.[11] He had the four furnished with arms, food, equipment, had them driven with the unit's car part of the way and ordered that their retreat be secured by his patrols. The officer did not rule out that Dayan, too, knew of the operation in advance. Moreover, the four now refuse to talk upon an explicit order from Arik [Sharon], perhaps approved by Dayan. A campaign is being organized against me because I revealed their identity (to the press). Arik is shouting that I have exposed the men to revenge in the case that they will fall prisoners while fighting in the army at any future time. (11 March 1955, 834)

The four are ready to confess on the condition that they will be guaranteed an amnesty. (13 March 1955, 840)

In the thirties we restrained the emotions of revenge and we educated the public to consider revenge as an absolutely negative impulse. Now, on the contrary, we justify the system of reprisal out of pragmatic considerations . . . we have eliminated the mental and moral brakes on this instinct and made it possible . . . to uphold revenge as a moral value. This notion is held by large parts of the public in general, the masses of youth in particular, but it has crystalized and reached *the value of a sacred principle* in [Sharon's] battalion which becomes the revenge instrument of the State.[12] (31 March 1955, 840)

The British ambassador, Nichols, expressed . . . his surprise at the release of the four. According to him, Jordanians arrested the murderer of the couple in Ajur. . . . What a contrast between their step and the shameful procedure adopted by us! . . . Kesseh [the Secretary General of Mapai] learned from his son [a senior army officer] that the operation had been carried out with the full knowledge of the army, on all levels, including the Chief of Staff and in it were involved senior officers. (28 March 1955, 870)

At a meeting of Mapai's secretariat on January 11, 1961, six years later, Sharett returned to this haunting episode.

The phenomenon that has prevailed among us for years and years is that of insensitivity to acts of wrong . . . to moral corruption. . . . For us, an act of wrong is in itself nothing serious; we wake up to it only if the threat of a crisis or a grave result—the loss of a position, the loss of power or influence—is involved. We don't have a moral approach to moral problems but a pragmatic approach to moral problems. . . . Once, Israeli soldiers murdered a number of Arabs for reasons of blind revenge . . . and no conclusion was drawn from that, no one was demoted, no one was removed from office. Then there was Kafr Qasim* . . . those responsible have not drawn any conclusions. This, however, does not mean that public opinion, the army, the police, have drawn no conclusion, their conclusion was that Arab blood can be freely shed. And then came the amnesty for those of Kafr Qasim, and some conclusions could be drawn again, and I could go on like this. (11 January 1961, 769)

All this must bring about revulsion in the sense of justice and honesty in public opinion; it must make the State appear in the eyes of the world as a savage state that does not recognize the principles of justice as they have been established and accepted by contemporary society.

*See Appendix 2.

7

The Lavon Affair:
Terrorism to Coerce the West _____

ONE: Start immediate action to prevent or postpone Anglo-Egyptian Agreement. Objectives are: one, cultural and information centers; two, economic institutions; three, cars of British representatives and other Britons; four, whichever target whose sabotage could bring about a worsening of diplomatic relations. TWO. Inform us on possibilities of action in Canal Zone. THREE. Listen to us every day at 7 o'clock on wavelength G.

This coded cable was sent to the Israeli spy ring which had been planted in Egypt many months before it was activated in July 1954. The ring originally was to serve as a fifth column during the next war. The cable was preceded by oral instructions given by Colonel Benjamin Givli, head of Israel's military intelligence, to an officer headed for Cairo to join the ring. These instructions were:

[Our goal is] to break the West's confidence in the existing [Egyptian] regime....The actions should cause arrests, demonstrations, and expressions of revenge. The Israeli origin should be totally covered while attention should be shifted to any other possible factor. The purpose is to prevent economic and military aid from the West to Egypt. The choice of the precise objectives to be sabotaged will be left to the men on the spot, who should evaluate the possible consequences of each action . . . in terms of creating commotion and public disorders.[13]

These orders were carried out between July 2 and July 27, 1954, by the network which was composed of about ten Egyptian Jews under the command of Israeli agents. Negotiations were at their height between Cairo and London for the evacuation of the Canal Zone, and between Cairo and Washington for arms supplies and other aid in connection with a possible U.S.-Egyptian alliance. British and American cultural and informational centers, British-owned cinemas, but also Egyptian public buildings (such as post offices) were bombed in Cairo and Alexandria. Suspicion was shifted to the Muslim Brothers, opponents of Nasser's regime. The Israeli ring was finally discovered and broken up on July 27, when one of its members was caught after a bomb exploded in his pocket in Alexandria.

On that same date Sharett, who knew nothing about the ring, was informed of the facts, and he began to collect evidence on the responsibilities of defense ministry and army officials. He did nothing beyond this, however, until October 5, when Cairo officially announced the imminent trial of the arrested saboteurs. Sharett then fully supported the campaign launched by Israel to present the case as an anti-Jewish frame-up by the Egyptian regime. On December 13, two days after the trial opened in Cairo, the prime minister denounced in the Knesset "the plot . . . and the show trial . . . against a group of Jews . . . victims of false accusations."* His party's paper, *Davar*, went as far as to accuse the Egyptian government of *"a Nazi-inspired policy."* Horror stories of confessions extracted from the accused under torture circulated in the Israeli and international media. Sharett knew all this to be untrue. "In reality," he wrote in his diary on January 2, 1955, "except for the first two days of their arrest, when there was some beating, the treatment of our men was absolutely decent and humane." But publicly, he kept silent—when he did not himself join the massive anti-Nasser chorus. Even the members of the cabinet, the president of the state, not to speak of the press, were not officially informed until some time in February, when rumors exploded on each street corner in Israel. Then the true story came out, that the government propaganda had been false from beginning to end, that the terrorist ring was indeed planted in Egypt by the Israelis and the only frame-up in question was the one invented against Egypt by the Sharett administration.

By the time the trial was over—two of the accused were condemned to death and executed, eight were condemned to long terms of imprisonment, while the three Israeli commanders of the operation succeeded in fleeing from Egypt and the fourth committed suicide—other important facts became known to the prime minister. The technical question of who actually gave the order to activate the ring on a certain date was not to be cleared up until six years later, when a fourth or fifth inquiry commission finally and definitely exonerated Lavon from that responsibility, and established that Dayan, Peres, Givli and other, minor, "security" aides had forged documents and falsified testimonies in order to bring about the incrimination of the minister of defense. In 1954-55, Sharett anticipated the findings of that commission, figuring that the entire leadership of the security establishment was guilty of the affair. For him, the question of who gave the order was secondary to the necessity of pronouncing a judgment on the ideology and politics of Israel's terrorism. Therefore, while he had no doubts about the guilt of the Dayan-Peres-Givli clique, to him Lavon's *political* responsibility was also inescapable.

[People] ask me if I am convinced that "he gave the order?" . . . but let us assume that Givli has acted without instructions . . . doesn't the moral responsibility lie

*See Appendix 4.

all the same on Lavon, who has constantly preached for acts of madness and taught the army leadership the diabolic lesson of how to set the Middle East on fire, how to cause friction, cause bloody confrontations, sabotage targets and property of the Powers [and perform] acts of despair and suicide? (10 January 1955, 639)

At this point, Sharett could have changed the history of the Middle East. Had he spoken frankly and directly to public opinion, which was deeply troubled by the events in Egypt—the arrests, the trial, the executions, the contradicting rumors, the climate of intrigue surrounding the "Affair,"— tearing up the mask of secrecy, denouncing those who were responsible, exposing his true convictions in regard to Israel's terroristic ideologies and orientations, proposing an alternative, he could have created for himself the conditions in which to use the formal powers that he possessed to make a radical housecleaning in the security establishment. The impact of such an act would have probably been considerable not only in Israel itself but also in the Arab world, especially in Egypt. The downfall of Lavon on one hand and of the Ben Gurionist gang, headed by Dayan and Peres, on the other hand might have blocked Ben Gurion's return to power, and in the longer range, the Sinai-Suez war. Events since then would have taken a different course.[14]

As it was, though, the prime minister had neither the courage nor the temperament required for such an action. Moreover, he always feared that his "moderate" convictions would expose him to accusations of defeatism by the activists of aggressive Zionism. Thus, he took cover behind a variety of pretexts aimed at justifying his passivity even to himself, while in his heart he knew that his objective compliance with the rules of the game imposed by his enemies would boomerang, in the end, against his own career. An open admission of the facts, he tormentedly argued, could be damaging to the people on trial in Cairo; or it could damage Israel's image in the world; or it could bring about a split in the Mapai party, to whose leadership Lavon and Ben Gurion as well as he belonged, causing it to lose its majority in the next elections. Inevitably, he ended up entangled in the plots woven around him by the opposing factions in the government, the army and the party. By mid-February, he had no other choice but to acquiesce to the unspoken ultimatum of Ben Gurion's men and appeal to the Old Man to reenter the cabinet as minister of defense in Lavon's place.

By January 1955, Sharett was well aware that the "Affair" was being used by Lavon and his friends on one hand, the Ben Gurionists on the other, and such extremist pro-militarist factions as Ahdut Ha'avoda[15]—to bring into the open the conflict between the "activist" line and the prime minister's "moderate" politics. He was informed also that Dayan was attempting to organize a coup d'etat and that Ben Gurion had given it his support. Other persons who had been approached (mainly from among Mapai's younger militants) had rejected the idea of a change of leadership through violence.[16] Dayan wanted to avoid at any cost being exposed by the investigation committee nominated by Sharett as one of those actually responsible for the "Affair." Lavon, on the other hand, threatened to commit suicide if the commission declared him guilty of having given the order.

Teddy [Kollek] painted a horrifying picture of the relations at the top of the security establishment. The Minister of Defense is completely isolated—none of his collaborators speaks to him. During the inquiry, these collaborators [e.g., Peres, Dayan and a number of senior Ministry officials and army officers] plotted to blacken his name and trap him. They captured the man who came from abroad, [the commander of the unit in Egypt Avraham Zeidenberg, also known as "Paul Frank," "Elad," or "the third man"] who escaped from Egypt...instructed him in detail how to answer, including how to lie to the investigators, and coordinated the testimonies so as to close the trap on Lavon. Teddy is convinced that Lavon must go immediately. Givli, too, must be dismissed, but Dayan, however, should not be touched for the time being. (9 January 1954, 637)

I would never have imagined that we could reach such a horrible state of poisoned relations, the unleashing of the basest instincts of hate and revenge and mutual deceit at the top of our most glorious Ministry [of Defense].

I walk around as a lunatic, horror-stricken and lost, completely helpless . . . what should I do? What should I do? (10 January 1954, 639)

Isser [Harel, head of the Shin Bet, stung at the time because the "Affair" had been conducted by the military intelligence, without coordination with his organization] told me hair-raising stories about a conversation which Givli initiated with him proposing to abduct Egyptians not only from the Gaza Strip but also in Cyprus and Europe. He also proposed a crazy plan to blow up the Egyptian Embassy in Amman in case of death sentences in the Cairo trial. (14 January 1955, 654)

To Aharon Barkatt, then secretary general of Mapai, Sharett painted the following picture of Israel's security establishment:

Dayan was ready to hijack planes and kidnap [Arab] officers from trains, but he was shocked by Lavon's suggestion about the Gaza Strip. Maklef [who preceded Dayan as Chief of Staff] demanded a free hand to murder Shishakly but he was shaken when Lavon gave him a crazy order concerning the Syrian DMZ. (25 January 1955, 682)

He [Lavon] inspired and cultivated the negative adventuristic trend in the army and preached the doctrine that not the Arab countries but the Western Powers are the enemy, and the only way to deter them from their plots is through direct actions that will terrorize them. (26 January 1955, 685)

Peres shares the same ideology: he wants to frighten the West into supporting Israel's aims.

8

Nasser: Coexistence with Israel is Possible
Ben Gurion's Reply: Operation Gaza _____

Commenting on Israel's terrorist actions in Egypt, a U.S. embassy official in Cairo concluded on February 8, 1955 that "Sharett does not have control of the matters if such mad actions can be carried out."[17]

The State Department, the prime minister noted, feared subsequent Israeli provocations to sabotage U.S. relations with the Arab world following the signing of the Ankara-Baghdad pact. The American administration therefore attempted to move simultaneously in two directions in order to save what may be saved in the given situation: it placed pressure on Nasser to negotiate some kind of agreement with the Sharett government, and it offered the Zionist state a security pact. The Israeli premier noted that Kermit Roosevelt Jr. of the CIA was working on the creation of contacts between Israel and Egypt, and that he, Sharett, would nominate Yigael Yadin as his representative. (21 January 1955, 675)

[I met with] Roger Baldwin, the envoy of the U.S. League of Human Rights who visited Cairo. . . . Nasser talked to him about Israel, saying that he is not among those who want to throw Israel into the Mediterranean. He believes in coexistence with Israel and knows that negotiations will open some day. (25 January 1955, 680)

Cable from Eban . . . the U.S. is ready to sign an agreement with us whereby we shall make a commitment not to extend our borders by force, it will commit itself to come to our aid if we were attacked. (28 January 1955, 691)

Teddy [Kollek] brought a message from Isser's [head of the Security Services] men in Washington. The partners [the CIA] renew their suggestion for a meeting with Nasser, who does not regard the initiative of the meeting canceled because of the outcome of the trial. . . . He is as willing to meet us as before and the initiative is now up to Israel. (10 February 1955, 716)

[In regard to Washington's proposals for a U.S.-Israel security pact] I cabled Eban that we are willing to accept a clause which obliges us not to extend our borders by force, but we should in no way commit ourselves to desist from any hostile acts because this would mean closing the door on any possibility to carry out reprisal actions. (14 February 1955, 726)

This last phrase indicates that the news of the American proposals, and of possible negotiations between Sharett and Nasser had spread rapidly in the security establishment. The pressures on Sharett were stepped up. On February 17, Ben Gurion accepted the premier's invitation to return to the government as minister of defense. Quoting his landlady, Sharett noted on that day in his diary "that is the end of peace and quiet." Ten days later, in fact

> Ben Gurion arrived . . . with . . . the Chief of Staff, who was carrying rolled-up maps. I understood at once what would be the subject of the conversation. . . . The Chief of Staff's proposal was to hit an Egyptian army base at the entrance to the city of Gaza. . . . [He] estimated that the enemy losses would be about ten . . . and that we have to be prepared for a few victims on our side. Ben Gurion insisted that the intention is not to kill but only to destroy buildings. If the Egyptians run away under the shock of the attack, there may be no bloodshed at all.

> I approved the plan. The act of infiltration near Rehovot—30km from the border of the Gaza Strip—shocked the public and a lack of reaction is unacceptable. . . . In my heart I was sorry that the reprisal would be attributed [by the public] to Ben Gurion. After all, I did authorize a reprisal action . . . when Ben Gurion was away from the government, and it was purely by chance that the operation did not take place. I would have approved this one, too, regardless of Ben Gurion being the Minister of Defense. (27 February 1955, 799–800)

> I am shocked. The number [of Egyptian victims (39 dead and 30 wounded, including a 7-year-old boy,)] changes not only the dimensions of the operation but its very substance; it turns it into an event liable to cause grave political and military complications and dangers. . . . The army spokesman, on instructions from the Minister of Defense, delivered a false version to the press: a unit of ours, after having been attacked supposedly inside our territory, returned the fire and engaged a battle which later developed as it did. Who will believe us? (1 March 1955, 804)

It was the same old story: hit and run and try to fool the world—

> The embassies should be instructed to condemn Egypt and not to be on the defensive. . . . Now there will be a general impression that while we cry out over our isolation and the dangers to our security, we initiate aggression and reveal ourselves as being bloodthirsty and aspiring to perpetrate mass massacres . . . it is possible that this outburst will be interpreted as the result of the army and the nation's outrage against the Powers' policy of ignoring the security of their state and will prevent the continuation of that policy to the bitter end. We, at least, have to make sure that this will be the common impression. . . . I dictated a briefing for the embassies. . . . It is desirable that the press should express the following: (a) Our public opinion had been agitated by the penetration of an Egyptian gang into a densely populated area and its attack on public transportation; (b) It seems that the clash developed into a serious battle as the exchange of fire was going on; (c) Egypt always claims that it is in a state of war

with Israel which it demonstrates by acts such as blockade and murders—and if there is a state of war, these are the results; (d) This event cannot be detached from the general background of the feeling of isolation which prevails in Israel in view of the West's alliances with the Arab states . . . the most recent example of which is the Iraq-Turkey Pact whose anti-Israeli goals are particularly evident.

The last argument (d) needs very cautious handling in the sense that it should not be attributed to us and should be confided only to the most loyal [commentators] who must be warned not to appear inspired by our sources.

When I wrote these things [the instructions to the embassies] I still didn't know how crushing is the evidence-that was already published, refuting our official version. The huge amounts of arms and explosives, the tactics of the attack, the blocking and mining of the roads . . . the precise coordination of the attack. Who would be foolish enough to believe that such a complicated operation could "develop" from a casual and sudden attack on an Israeli army unit by an Egyptian unit? . . .

I am tormented by thoughts as to whether this is not my greatest failure as Prime Minister. Who knows what will be the political and security consequence? (1 March 1955, 804-805)

One of the immediate and inevitable consequences was the following:

Yesterday . . . there was a conversation between [Salah] Gohar [the chief Egyptian representative to the mixed armistice commission] and [Joseph] Tkoa. The Egyptian representative informed [Tkoa] immediately that right after the previous meeting [which took place immediately following the Gaza attack] . . . Nasser told him . . . that he had had a personal contact with Israel's Prime Minister and that there were good chances that things would develop in a positive way, but then came the attack on Gaza, and naturally now . . . it's off.

Lawson [U.S. Ambassador] thinks that the reason for the warning and the threats [from Arab countries] is fear which has seized the Arab World due to Ben Gurion's comeback. The Gaza attack is interpreted as signalling a decision on our part to attack on all fronts. The Americans, too, are afraid that it will lead to a new conflagration in the Middle East which will blow up all their plans. Therefore, they wish to obtain from us a definite commitment that similar actions will not be repeated. (12 March 1955, 837)

But it was precisely to prevent a similar commitment that Ben Gurion rejoined the government, and he had no intention of changing his mind. On the contrary, on March 25, less than a month after the attack on Gaza, he proposed to the cabinet that Israel proceed to *occupy the Gaza Strip*, this time for good. The discussion lasted five whole days and ended with the ministers divided between the opponents of the proposal, headed by Sharett, and Ben Gurion's supporters. With five votes in favor, nine against it, and two abstentions, the plan was rejected, or perhaps simply postponed. The security pact offered by the U.S., however, had to be rejected, because—as Dayan explained in April 1955—"it would put handcuffs on our military freedom of action." He went into a detailed explanation on May 26, during a meeting with Israel's ambassadors in Washington (Abba Eban), Paris (Ya'acov Tsur) and London (Eliahu Eilat). The conversation was reported to Sharett later by Ya'acob Herzog and Gideon Raphael:

We do not need (Dayan said) a security pact with the U.S.: such a pact will only constitute an obstacle for us. We face no danger at all of an Arab advantage of force for the next 8-10 years. Even if they receive massive military aid from the West, we shall maintain our military superiority thanks to our infinitely greater capacity to assimilate new armaments. The security pact will only handcuff us and deny us the freedom of action which we need in the coming years. Reprisal actions which we couldn't carry out if we were tied to a security pact are our vital lymph . . . they make it possible for us to maintain a high level of tension among our population and in the army. Without these actions we would have ceased to be a combative people and without the discipline of a combative people we are lost. We have to cry out that the Negev is in danger, so that young men will go there. . . .

The conclusions from Dayan's words are clear: This State has no international obligations, no economic problems, the question of peace is nonexistent. . . . It must calculate its steps narrow-mindedly and live on its sword. It must see the sword as the main, if not the only, instrument with which to keep its morale high and to retain its moral tension. Toward this end it may, no—it *must*— invent dangers, and to do this it must adopt the method of provocation-and-revenge. . . . And above all—let us hope for a new war with the Arab countries, so that we may finally get rid of our troubles and acquire our space. (Such a slip of the tongue: Ben Gurion himself said that it would be worth while to pay an Arab a million pounds to start a war.) (26 May 1955, 1021)

On August 14, a U.S. Quaker leader, Elmer Jackson, on a visit to Jerusalem after a meeting in Cairo with Egyptian Foreign Minister Mahmoud Fawzi, told Sharett that Nasser was still interested in normalizing relations with Israel. On October 7, the Egyptian president himself said to *New York Times* special envoy Kenneth Love: "No Arab says today that we should destroy Israel."[18] But Israel had already made its decisions.[19]

9

Disperse the
Palestinian Refugees...   _____

One important reason for the insistence with which Israel pursued its retaliation policy was the desire of the Zionist ruling establishment to exert permanent pressure on the Arab states to remove the Palestinian refugees of the 1948 war from the proximity of the armistice lines, and to disperse them through the Arab world. This was not due, in the early fifties, to military considerations: as we have seen, and as Dayan's above quotation clearly demonstrates, the Israeli government was more interested in the heightening of border tensions than in their elimination. Furthermore, its lack of concern for the security of the Jewish border population was as cynical as its own promotion of a sensation of danger among the settlers through provocation and false propaganda. Moreover, in those years no organized Palestinian resistance movement existed. It was all too obvious that the low level of guerrilla-type activities permitted by the Arab regimes was intended more to reduce the tensions created inside their countries by the presence of the refugees, and to keep the issue on the agenda in the international arena, than to prepare for a war of liberation in Palestine.[20] But the presence of the Palestinian refugees along the armistice lines—in Gaza and the West Bank—was not only a constant reminder of the illegitimacy of Israel's territorial conquests in 1948-49 and of its violation of UN resolutions calling for repatriation, it was also a living, physical landmark along borders which Israel had no intention of accepting as definite limits to its territorial expansion. In other words, as long as masses of Palestinians were still concentrated on Palestinian soil, the Israeli rulers argued, there was both the risk of international pressure in support of their claim to return to their homes, and little likelihood for international permission for Israel to cancel the geopolitical concept of Palestine entirely, substituting it with that of "Eretz-Israel."

It must be underlined at this point that Sharett's position on the Palestinian question did not differ, except regarding the use of *military* methods to disperse them, from that of the "activists." He had totally rejected Count Bernadotte's repeated pleas in 1948 for a return of the refugees to their homes (Folke Bernadotte *To Jerusalem*, London, 1951). A year later, he ridiculed the position of the General Zionist Party in favor of a Palestinian independent state in the West Bank and against an agreement with King Abdullah on the division of the West Bank between

Israel and Jordan *(Divrei, Haknesset*, Jerusalem, 1949). In his *Diary* there
are numerous references to negotiations attempted by his senior aides at
the foreign ministry with Arab representatives or exiles aimed at resettling
the Palestinians in countries such as Libya, Syria or Iraq. (Among others,
Mustafa Abdul Mun'im, Deputy Secretary General of the Arab League is
quoted by Sharett on May 23, 1954, as having affirmed that "the refugees
should be settled in the neighboring countries, or, if capital is available, in
Sinai.") On June 30, 1954, Sharett met with two representatives of a Union
of Palestinian Refugees, Aziz Shehadeh from Jaffa and Mahmud Yahia
from Tantura, in regard to the payment of compensation. Finally, on May
28, 1955, Sharett's ideas on the question of the Palestinian refugees were
unequivocally expressed in his instructions to Israel's ambassadors in
connection with the Security Pact offered to Israel by the U.S., which the
foreign minister suspected might include some conditions: "There may be
an attempt to reach peace by pressuring us to make concessions on the
question of territory and the refugees. I warned [the ambassadors] against
any thought of the possibility of returning a few tens of thousands of
refugees, *even at the price of peace.*" And this was the *"liberal"* Zionist
leader who claimed to be an expert on Arab affairs because he had lived for
two years, during his adolescence, in an Arab village in the West Bank;
because he knew Arabic; because he had lived in Syria during his military
service in the Turkish army. On the whole, his attitude toward the
Palestinians is well illustrated by a note in his *Diary* on November 15, 1953.
It refers to a report made that day to the cabinet meeting by Colonel
Yitzhak Shani, then chief military governor of the Arab minority in Israel.
(As is obvious, those whom Sharett calls infiltrators were forcefully
expelled Palestinian Arabs trying to return to their home villages or to re-
establish contacts with their families who remained under Israeli rule.)

In the last three years [Shani reported] 20,000 infiltrators settled in Israel, in
addition to 30,000 who returned immediately after the war. . . . Only because
these 20,000 have not been given permanent documents has the brake been put
on the flow of infiltration directed toward settlement. To abolish the military
government would mean to open the border areas to undisturbed infiltration
and to increasing penetration toward the interior of the country. Even as things
are, around 18,000 Arabs in Galilee are in possession of permanent permits to
move freely around but only to the West and the South and not toward the
North and the East. . . . It is true that the troublesome problem of the evacuees
must be liquidated through a permanent resettlement, but the evacuees firmly
refuse to settle on land belonging to refugees who are on the other side of the
border. . . . Even when stone houses are built for them, they refuse to settle in
them if they are built on absentee land. . . . The Arabs who continue to live on
their land enjoy advantages, since their production costs are much lower than
those of the Jews. In addition they are exempt from spending money and
engaging manpower for vigilance, as the infiltrators don't touch their property
. . . . It may be assumed that after this lecture the "General Zionists" demand that

the military government be abolished would finally be silenced. (15 November 1953, 150)

Throughout 1953-54 Sharett periodically referred in his diary to proposals made by Ben Gurion, Dayan, Lavon and others to present Egypt with an ultimatum: either it evacuates all the Palestinian refugees from Gaza and disperses them inside Egypt, or else. The description of the Cabinet discussion in the last week of March 1955 on Ben Gurion's demand for the occupation of Gaza, offers more details:

> The Defense Minister's proposal is that Israel declare invalid the armistice agreement with Egypt, and thus resume its "right" to renew the (1948-49) war....I have condemned the twisted logic in Ben Gurion's reliance on the violation of the armistice agreement by Egypt, in order to justify the declaration on our part that this agreement does not exist any more and thus we are allowed to resume the war. . . . Let us assume that there are 200,000 Arabs [in the Gaza Strip]. Let us assume that half of them will run or will be made to run to the Hebron Hills. Obviously they will run away without anything and shortly after they establish for themselves some stable environment, they will become again a riotous and homeless mob. It is easy to imagine the outrage and hate and bitterness and the desire for revenge that will animate them. . . . And we shall still have 100,000 of them in the Strip, and it is easy to imagine what means we shall resort to in order to repress them and what waves of hatred we shall create again and what kind of headlines we shall receive in the international press. The first round would be: Israel aggressively invades the Gaza Strip. The second: Israel causes again the terrified flight of masses of Arab refugees. (27 March 1955, 865)

In yet another six-hour cabinet meeting Sharett continues his arguments:

> What we succeeded in achieving . . . in 1948, cannot be repeated whenever we desire it. Today we must accept our existing frontiers and try to relax the tensions with our neighbors to prepare the ground for peace and strengthen our relations with the Powers. . . . Finally I proved that the occupation of the Gaza Strip will not resolve any security problem, as the refugees . . . will continue to constitute the same trouble, and even more so, as their hate will be rekindled . . . by the atrocities that we shall cause them to suffer during the occupation. (29 March 1955, 873)

> Ben Gurion's speech was . . . full of anger against those who disagree with him and who are in his opinion incapable of seeing the fatal forecast and cannot understand that we can only be delivered by daring action, if it will be performed in time, before the opportunity is missed. . . . The problem of the refugees is indeed a pain in the neck, but nevertheless we shall chase them to Jordan. (ibid., 874-875)

I expressed my doubts in regard to the [much publicized by Israel] growth of Egypt's military strength, seeing that this year all the energies of the [Egyptian] army have been absorbed in domestic conflicts and rivalries. . . . About 500 officers, among the best in the Egyptian forces, left the military services [after Nasser replaced Neguib] and passed to administrative and political activities. (30 March 1955)

But Israel's worldwide campaign had nothing whatever to do with the true facts:

Ben Gurion [in the cabinet meeting] declared that Nasser is the most dangerous enemy of Israel and is plotting to destroy her. . . . It is not clear where he gets this confidence that [enables him] to express [this] so definitely and decisively as if it were based on solid facts. (24 April 1955)

It was simply directed to mobilize international opinion against Egypt, and prepare a favorable ground for Israel's imminent military aggression. At the same time, however, Israeli officials were instructed to convince Western governments that the instability of Nasser's regime did not make it worthy of Western aid and support. As always when their end justified the means, Israel's rulers were not at all concerned about the contradiction between their parallel campaigns. To prove Nasser's weakness they resorted to testimonies by Egyptians:

Gideon Raphael . . . reported on . . . an interesting meeting with one of the major Egyptian capitalists, Aboud Pasha. . . . Aboud turned out to be a close friend of Nasser. It seems that he conserved and even strengthened his status under the new regime which is an enemy of capitalism. . . . According to Aboud, Nasser's position is unstable in his own ranks. He is constantly nervous and does not know whom to please first. The leadership of the group is divided and conflicts explode between the officers, each of whom leans on the support of a different corps—the air force, the navy, ground forces. The situation is very instable and it is difficult to know what will happen. (31 July 1955, 1100)

as well as to new attempts at subversion:

I sat with Josh Palmon . . . to hear a report on the continuation of the negotiations with the leaders of the Sudanese *Umma* party. . . . One of them will visit Israel soon. Some more possibilities of developing commercial connections between us and them. It is necessary to detach Sudan from economic dependence upon Egypt, and from its sphere of influence.

We are maintaining contacts with Wafd [rightist, nationalist, anti-Nasser Party] exiles in London. (3 October 1955)

The Eisenhower administration seemed divided. State Department pro-

10

... and Topple
Nasser's Regime _____

At the same cabinet meeting Ben Gurion, according to Sharett's *L*

> Tried to prove that Egypt aspires to dominate Africa, westwards to Mc
> and southwards to South Africa where one day the blacks will get u
> massacre the two million whites and then subject themselves to Egypt's
> authority. . . . Nasser, [he said] will probably not react to the occupation
> Gaza Strip because his regime is based solely on the army, and if he tries t
> back he will be defeated and his regime will collapse. The Arab Stat
> probably not come to Nasser's aid anyway. Finally, the Western powers w
> react . . . militarily. England will not invade the Negev—"and if she will, w
> fight and throw her out in disgrace. . . ." Our force is in the accomplishm
> facts—this is the only way for us to become a political factor which ha
> taken into consideration. This is the right moment because the Arab w
> divided and Egypt has not yet signed an agreement with the U.S. or Ei
> (ibid.)

To prevent an alliance between the West and the Arab world, esp
with the most important Arab country—Egypt—was (and was to r
Israel's main goal. This had nothing to do with Israel's security.
contrary, Ben Gurion's policy was directed at *preventing* guarantee
being imposed on the Zionist state by the U.S. Such guarantees
necessarily imply the achievement of a minimum agreement betwee
and the Arab world (definition of the borders, a "face-saving" solui
the Palestinian refugees). The basic motivation was also clearly sta
use of force was "the only way" for Israel to become a hegemonic p
the region, possibly in alliance with the West. Nasser had to be elir
not because his regime constituted a danger for Israel, but beca
alliance between the West and his prestigious leadership in the thirc
and in the Middle East, would inevitably lead to a peace agreemen
in turn would cause the Zionist state to be relativized as just on
region's national societies.

That Nasser's regime did not constitute any danger to Israel's e:
was well known at the time to the Israelis. Sharett noted:

Arab elements, according to Sharett, were still pressing for a Western-Arab alliance in the Middle East, and considered an agreement between Washington and Cairo essential to the security and stability of the region, in the words of Israel's foreign minister. But Israeli pressures were increasingly bearing fruit. After years of contacts and negotiations, Egyptian requests for defensive armaments resulted in no more than, as Mohammed Hassanein Heykal later disclosed, a personal present made to General Neguib in the form of a decorative pistol to wear at ceremonies, and this while Israel's military aggression was growing more brazen from day to day. No economic aid to speak of was reaching Egypt from the West. And John Foster Dulles' commitment to help Egypt in the construction of the Aswan Dam had faded into thin air. Cairo was humiliated, while Western verbal regrets after the devastating Israeli attack on Gaza did not seem to have affected in any way Israel's preparations for an all-out war. Ben Gurion made a public speech on August 8 in which he criticized Sharett's policy as being aimed only at pleasing the gentiles and pointed towards the destruction of the state. He announced that from now on the foreign minister's duty will be none else than to explain to the world the defense ministry's security policies. These factors contributed to extinguishing Cairo's last illusions. By the end of September 1955, Egypt signed an arms deal with Czechoslovakia intended to secure its survival and self-defense.

On October 1st

Teddy [Kollek] brought in a classified cable from Washington. Our "partner" named [in code] "Ben" [Kermit Roosevelt of the CIA] . . . describes the terrible confusion prevailing in the State Department under the shock of the Nasser-Czech "i.e., Russian" deal. (Henry) Byroade and all the others who were in favor of U.S. support to Egypt lost their say completely. He adds: "We are surprised at your silence." When our man asked for the meaning of these words, and whether we are expected to go to war, the answer was: "If, when the Soviet arms arrive, you will hit Egypt—no one will protest." (1 October 1955, 1182)

In the cabinet meeting on October 3 at one stage Ben Gurion declared:

"If they really get Migs . . . I will support their bombing! We can do it!" I understood that he read the cable from Washington. The wild seed has fallen on fertile ground. (3 October 1955)

Isser [Harel, Shin Bet chief] likewise concludes that the U.S. is hinting to us that as far as they are concerned, we have a free hand and God bless us if we act audaciously. . . . Now . . . the U.S. is interested in toppling Nasser's regime, . . . but it does not dare at the moment to use the methods it adopted to topple the leftist government of Jacobo Arbenz in Guatemala [1954] and of Mossadegh in Iran [1953]. . . . It prefers its work to be done by Israel.

Hence, Isser proposes seriously and pressingly . . . that we carry out our plan for the occupation of the Gaza Strip now. . . . The situation is changed and there are other reasons which determine that it is "time to act." First the discovery of oil near the Strip . . . its defense requires dominating the Strip—this alone is worth dealing with the troublesome question of the refugees. Second, Egypt's betrayal of the West. This fact eliminates the danger of an armed intervention of the Powers against us. (ibid., 1186)

Precisely one year later Dayan's troops occupied the Gaza Strip, Sinai, and the Straits of Tiran and were arrayed along the shore of the Suez Canal to watch the spectacular French and British aerial bombardments of Ismailia and Suez, accompanied by the rapid landing of troops in the Canal Zone. Six months before, as a result of a personal decision of Ben Gurion, Sharett had been eliminated from the government. The premiership had been resumed by the Old Man in November 1955, one month after the U.S. "green light" for an Israeli invasion of Egypt. A vicious whisper campaign had been mounted, to present the foreign minister as incapable of obtaining for Israel the arms necessary for its defense. The atmosphere surrounding Sharett's departure is significant:

[Around] the table [in the Cabinet meeting] they all sat in silence. None of my colleagues raised his head to look at me. No one got up to shake my hand, despite everything. It was as if all their mental capacities were paralyzed, as if the freedom of movement was banned from their bodies, the freedom of expression was taken away from their hearts and the freedom of independent action from their consciences. They sat heavy and staring in their silence. Thus I crossed the whole length of the meeting room, and left. (18 June 1956)

In the next months the U.S. authorized France to divert to Israel Mirage planes which were already earmarked for NATO. At the moment of the Suez offensive the U.S. feigned surprise, and even indignation. But it made a clear distinction between England and France, the beaten rivals in the inter-imperialist struggle for influence in the Middle East, and Israel. The immediate retreat of Britain and France from Egypt was requested by President Eisenhower within a matter of hours. Israel's withdrawal from Gaza and Sinai was pushed through only four months later and then only thanks to heavy Soviet pressure which threatened to submerge the West in unforeseen complications to world peace. Israel, with the CIA authorization in its pocket, was granted the mitigating circumstances of "security needs" in world opinion's judgment on that criminal war. The precedent had thus been set, and could only mean that the retreat from Gaza and Sinai was to be purely tactical, as the 1967 war later proved.

As a so-called moderate Zionist, Moshe Sharett's lifelong assumption had been that Israel's survival would be impossible without the support of the West, but that Western so-called morality as well as Western objective interests in the Middle East would never allow the West to support a

Jewish state which "behaves according to the laws of the jungle" and raises terrorism to the level of a sacred principle. To prominent Mapai leader David Hacohen, who declared himself convinced that the Israelis should behave in the Middle East as if they were crazy in order to terrorize the Arabs and blackmail the West, he replied: If we shall behave like madmen, we shall be treated as such—interned in a lunatic asylum and isolated from the world. But his adversaries proved him wrong, thereby dealing a crushing blow to his personality as well as to the very hypothesis of moderate Zionism. What they proved was that his supposedly rational assumption was not only fallacious but also unrealistic. In the final analysis the West, and in particular the U.S., let itself be frightened, or blackmailed, into supporting Israel's megalomanic ambitions, because an objective relationship of complicity already existed and because once pushed into the open this complicity proved capable of serving the cause of Western power politics in the region.[21] Just as Zionism, based on the de-Palestinization and the Judaization of Palestine, was intrinsically racist and immoral, thus the West, in reality, had no use for a Jewish state in the Middle East which *did not* behave according to the laws of the jungle, and whose terrorism *could not* be relied on as a major instrument for the oppression of the peoples of the region. There was a fatal but coherent logic in this newly acquired equation, which would determine the course of future events:

> I go on repeating to myself: nowadays admit that you are the loser! They showed much more daring and dynamism . . . they played with fire, and they won. Admit that the balance sheet of the Sinai war is positive. Moral evaluations apart, Israel's political importance in the world has grown enormously. . . . You remain alone. Only your son Coby is with you. The public, even your own public, does not share your position. On the contrary . . . the public now turns even against its "masters" and its bitterness against the retreat [from Sinai and Gaza] is developing into a tendency to change the political balance in this country in favour of Begin. (4 April 1957)

Operation Kibya

Ben Gurion's version of operation Kibya, broadcasted on Israeli Radio on 19 October 1953, as recorded by *Davar*, 20 October 1953.

(...)The [Jewish] border settlers in Israel, mostly refugees, people from Arab countries and survivors from the Nazi concentration camps, have, for years, been the target of(...)murderous attacks and had shown a great restraint. Rightfully, they have demanded that their government protect their lives and the Israeli government gave them weapons and trained them to protect themselves.

But the armed forces from Transjordan did not stop their criminal acts, until [the people in] some of the border settlements lost their patience and after the murder of a mother and her two children in Yahud, they attacked, last week, the village of Kibya across the border, that was one of the main centers of the murderers' gangs. Every one of us regrets and suffers when blood is shed anywhere and nobody regrets more than the Israeli government the fact that innocent people were killed in the retaliation act in Kibya. But all the responsibility rests with the government of Transjordan that for many years tolerated and thus encouraged attacks of murder and robbery by armed powers in its country against the citizens of Israel.

The government of Israel strongly rejects the ridiculous and fantastic version, as if 600 soldiers participated [in the action] against Kibya. We had conducted a thorough check and found out that not even the smallest army unit was missing from its base on the night of the attack on Kibya (emphasis ours).

APPENDIX 2

"And Then There Was Kafr Qasim..."

On the eve of the 1956 Sinai War, Israeli Brigadier Shadmi, the commander of a battalion on the Israeli-Jordanian border, ordered a night curfew imposed on the "minority" (Arab) villages under his command. These villages were inside the Israeli borders; thus, their inhabitants were Israeli citizens. According to the court records *(Judgements of the District Court*, The Military Prosecutor vs. Major Melinki, et. al.), Shadmi told the commander of a Frontier Guard unit, Major Melinki, that the curfew must be "extremely strict" and that "it would not be enough to arrest those who broke it—they must be shot." He added: "A dead man (or according to other evidence 'a few men') is better than the complications of detention."

The court recordings continue:

He (Melinki) informed the assembled officers that the war had begun, that their units were now under the command of the Israeli Defence Army, and that their task was to impose the curfew in the minority villages from 1700 to 0600, after informing the Mukhtars to this effect at 1630. With regard to the observation of the curfew, Melinki emphasized that it was forbidden to harm inhabitants who stayed in their homes, but that anyone found outside his home (or, according to other witnesses, anyone leaving his home, or anyone breaking the curfew) should be shot dead. He added that there were to be no arrests, and that if a number of people were killed in the night (according to other witnesses: it was desirable that a number of people should be killed as) this would facilitate the imposition of the curfew during succeeding nights.

... While he was outlining this series of orders, Major Melinki allowed the officers to ask him questions. Lieutenant Franknanthal asked him "What do we do with the dead?" (or, according to other witnesses "with the wounded?") Melinki replied: "Take no notice of them" (or, according to other evidence: "They must not be removed," or, according to a third witness: "There will not be any wounded.") Arieh Menches, a section leader, then asked "What about women and children?" to which Melinki replied "No sentimentality" (according to another witness: "They are to be treated like anyone else; the curfew covers them too.") Menches then asked a second question: "What about people returning from their work?" Here Alexandroni tried to intervene, but Melinki silenced him, and answered: "They are to be treated like anyone else" (according to another witness, he added: "It will be just too bad for them, as the Commander said.")

In the minutes of the meeting which were taken down and signed by Melinki a short time after he signed the series of orders, the following appears:

As from today, at 1700 hours, curfew shall be imposed in the minority villages until 0600 hours, and all who disobey this order will be shot dead.

After this psychological preparation, and the instructions given to the policemen-soldiers to "shoot to kill all who broke the curfew," the unit went out to the village of Kafr Qasim to start its work:

The first to be shot at the western entrance to the village were four quarrymen returning on bicycles from the places where they worked near Petah Tiqva and Ras al-Ain. A short time after the curfew began these four workmen came round the bend in the road pushing their bicycles. When they had gone some ten to fifteen metres along the road towards the school, they were shot from behind at close range, from the left. Two of the four (Ahmad Mahmud Freij and Ali Othman Taha, both 30 years old) were killed outright. The third (Muhammad Mahmud Freij, brother of Ahmad Freij) was wounded in the thigh and the forearm, while the fourth, Abdullah Samir Badir, escaped by throwing himself to the ground. The bicycle of the wounded man, Ahmad, fell on him and covered his body, and he managed to lie motionless throughout the bloody incidents that took place around him. Eventually he crawled into an olive grove and lay under an olive tree until morning. Abdullah was shot at again when he rolled from the road to the sidewalk, whereupon he sighed and pretended to be dead. After the two subsequent massacres, which took place beside him, he hid himself among a flock of sheep, whose shepherd had been killed, and escaped into the village with the flock. . . .

A short time after this killing a shepherd and his twelve year old son came back from the pasture with their flock. They approached the bend along the road from the Jewish colony of Masha. The flock went along the road as far as the village school, the shepherd throwing stones at sheep that had strayed to turn them back on to the Masha road. Two or three soldiers, standing by the bend, opened fire at close range on the shepherd and his son and killed them. Their names were Othman Abdullah Issa, aged 30, and his son Fathi Othman Abdullah Issa, aged twelve.

Note: The translation of the court proceedings appeared in *The Arabs in Israel* by Sabri Jiyris (Monthly Review, 1976). Jiyris sums up: "In the first hour of the curfew, between 5 and 6 PM, the men of the Israeli Frontier Guard killed forty-seven Arab citizens in Kafr Qasim."

"Soon the Singing Will Turn Into A Death Moan"

The following is excerpted from Meir Har-Tzion's *Diary*, published by Levin-Epstein, Ltd., Tel Aviv, 1969. It describes an Israeli raid in Gaza during the early 1950s.

The wide, dry riverbed glitters in the moonlight. We advance, carefully, along the mountain slope. Several houses can be seen. Bushes and shrubbery sway in the breeze, casting their shadows on the ground. In the distance we can see three lights and hear the sounds of Arab music coming out of the homes immersed in darkness. We split up into three groups of four men each. Two groups make their way to the immense refugee camp to the south of our position. The other group marches towards the lonely house in the flat area north of Wadi Gaza. We march forward, trampling over green fields, wading through water canals as the moon bathes us in its scintillating light. Soon, however, the silence will be shattered by bullets, explosions, and the screams of those who are now sleeping peacefully. We advance quickly and enter one of the houses—"Mann Haatha?" (Arabic for "Who's there?")

We leap towards the voices. Fearing and trembling, two Arabs are standing up against the wall of the building. They try to escape. I open fire. An earpiercing scream fills the air. One man falls to the ground, while his friend continues to run. Now we must act—we have no time to lose. We make our way from house to house as the Arabs scramble about in confusion. Machine guns rattle, their noise mixed with a terrible howling. We reach the main thoroughfare of the camp. The mob of fleeing Arabs grows larger. The other group attacks from the opposite direction. The thunder of hand grenades echoes in the distance. We receive an order to retreat. The attack has come to an end.

On the following morning, the headlines will read: "The refugee camp of Al-Burj near Gaza was attacked. The camp has been serving as a base for infiltrators into Israeli territory. Twenty people were killed and another twenty were wounded."

. . . A telephone line blocks our way. We cut it and continue. A narrow path leads along the slope of a hill. The column marches forward in silence. Stop! A few rocks roll down the hill. I catch sight of a man surveying the silence. I cock my rifle. Gibly crawls over to me, "Har, for God's sake, a knife!!" His clenched teeth glitter in the dark and his whole body is tight, his mind alert, "For God's sake," . . . I put my tommy down and unsheath my machete. We crawl towards the lone figure as he begins to sing a trilled Arab tune. Soon the singing will turn into a death moan. I am shaking, every muscle in my body is tense. This is my first experience with this type of weapon. Will I be able to do it?

We draw closer. There he stands, only a few meters in front of us. We leap. Gibly grabs him and I plunge the knife deep into his back. The blood pours over his striped cotton shirt. With not a second to lose, I react instinctively and stab him again. The body groans, struggles and then becomes quiet and still.

From an interview with Meir Har-Tzion, *Ha'aretz* weekly supplement, 9 November 1965:

"Pangs of conscience? No. Why should I have any?" The man's blue eyes open wide in amazement. "It's easy to kill a man with a rifle. You press the trigger and that's that. But a knife, why, that's something else—that's a real fight. Even if you are successful, you come close to death. The enemy's blade is as close as the air. It's a fantastic feeling. You realize you're a man."

The Lavon Affair

Moshe Sharett's public version of "The Lavon Affair" in his statement to Israel's Parliament (Divrei Ha-Knesset, the 514th meeting, 13 December 1954):

Honorable Chairman, members of the Knesset. The trial that started two days ago in Egypt against 13 Jews is disturbing everybody and brings about an emotional turmoil and deep bitterness in the country [Israel] and in the whole Jewish world. Indeed, it must cause concern and anxiety in the hearts of all justice-seeking people around the universe. The Committee for Foreign Affairs and Security has already dealt and will further deal with this serious issue. But at this stage I feel obliged to make a short announcement.

In my speech in the Knesset on November 15 I said "The uncontrolled behavior of Egypt . . . does not indicate . . . that its leadership . . . is seeking moderate approaches and peace. How far Egypt is from this spirit [of moderation and peace] can be learned from the plot woven in Alexandria—the show-trial which is being organized there against a group of Jews who became victims of false accusations of espionage, and who, it seems, are being threatened and tortured in order to extract from them confessions in imaginary crimes."

This gloomy assumption was verified and was revealed to be a cruel and shocking fact, by the declaration of the accused Victorin Ninyo in the military court in Cairo that was published this morning. [According to this declaration] she was tortured during the interrogation which preceded the trial and by that torture they extracted from her false confessions to crimes which did not happen.

The government of Israel strongly protests this practice, which revives in the Middle East the methods used by the Inquisition in the Middle Ages. The government of Israel strongly rejects the false accusations of the general Egyptian prosecution, which relegates to the Israeli authorities horrible deeds and diabolic conspiracies against the security and the international relations of Egypt.

From this stand we have protested many times in the past persecution and false accusations of Jews in various countries. We see in the innocent Jews accused by the Egyptian authorities of such severe crimes, victims of vicious hostility to the State of Israel and the Jewish people. If their crime is being Zionist and devoted to Israel, millions of Jews around the world share this crime. We do not think that the rulers of Egypt should be interested in being responsible for shedding Jewish blood. We call upon all those who believe in peace, stability and human relations among nations to prevent fatal injustice.

Israeli Newspaper Reveals Government's Attempt to Stop Publication of *Israel's Sacred Terrorism*

Following are major excerpts from an article by Israeli Member of the Knesset Uri Avneri, published in *Hoalam Hazeh*, September 23, 1980, entitled "Sharett's Diary for the Arabs."

The booklet uses quotations from Sharett's diary to illuminate eight affairs which took place during the fifties. Livia Rokach did clean work. All her quotations are real. She did not ever take them out of context, nor did she quote them in a way that contradicts the intention of the diary writer. To any person who is familiar with Israeli propaganda, such quotations may have a stunning effect . . .

Through the use of selective excerpts from Sharett's diary, her historical research deals in detail with the following affairs:

1. Retaliation activities

Quotations from Sharett show that these activities were never carried out in revenge or retaliation, as they were presented to be, but that they were the product of the premeditated policies of David Ben Gurion and Moshe Dayan. These policies aimed at heating the borders, as a preparation for war, and as a pretext to vacate and disperse Palestinian refugees who lived in camps close to the borders. Quotations from Sharett's book also reveal that President Yitzhak Ben Zvi hoped for an Egyptian attack to justify Israel's occupation of half of Sinai. Sharett reveals, furthermore, that the incidents on the Syrian border were also a result of an Israeli initiative. Sharett details at length the reasons behind the blood-bath committed by the 101 unit, under the command of Arik Sharon, in the village of Kibya, where fifty-six innocent Arab villagers were killed. He also recites how the government decided to publish a false communique, in which this event was portrayed as a partisan action carried out by civilian "settlers."

2. The plan for the occupation of Southern Syria

Sharett reveals that Ben Gurion, Dayan and Pinhas Lavon requested in February 1954 to exploit the toppling of the Syrian dictator, Adib Shishakly, by occupying southern Syria and annexing it to Israel. They also requested to buy a Syrian officer who would acquire power in Damascus and establish a pro-Israel puppet government. These things seem more actual today in light of the deteriorating position of Hafez al-Assad and Israeli declarations in this regard.

3. The intention to partition Lebanon

Sharett reveals that already in February 1954 Ben Gurion proposed a large Israeli operation to dismember the Lebanese state and to establish a Maronite-Christian state in one of its parts. Extended discussions were held as a result. Ben Gurion explicated the plan at length in a letter to Sharett, and Sharett answered in a long letter in which he opposed the plan vehemently. Ben Gurion was ready to invest large sums in bribing Christian leaders in Lebanon. Sharett also revealed that the chief of staff supported the plan of buying a Lebanese army officer who would be used as a puppet, and who would make it seem that the intervention of the Israeli army would be in response to his call for the liberation of Lebanon from Muslim subjugation. In the eyes of today's reader this plan seems an accurate blueprint for what took place in Lebanon after that—the civil war, the establishment of the Maronite enclave of Major Sa'd Haddad and labeling it "free Lebanon."

4. The Har-Tzion Affair

Sharett recites how Meir Har-Tzion of the 101 Unit murdered with his own hands five innocent Bedouin youth in revenge for the killing of his sister who crossed the Jordanian border during one of her hikes. Sharett recites, further, how Arik Sharon and Moshe Dayan covered over this abhorrent act, and how Ben Gurion foiled his decision to bring Har-Tzion and his friends to justice.

5. The Lavon Affair

Sharett describes at length the nasty business in Egypt. Livia Rokach appended to the book in which Sharett reveals the truth about the affair his own lies-filled speech in the Knesset in which he claimed that the accusations against those indicted in the Cairo trials were motivated by bloodlibel and antisemitism.

The Israeli reader who read the excerpts from Sharett's diary which were serialized in *Maariv*, or even the eight volumes of the diary themselves cannot be shocked by these revelations, in spite of their severity. However, the impact of such a publication abroad is bound to be sharper. Indeed, the lack of legal intervention by the Israeli Foreign Office prevented a wide spread dissemination of the booklet. The Arab-American organization that published the booklet does not have the means required to disseminate it widely, especially when faced with the conspiracy of silence imposed by the pro-Israel American media....

NOTES

1. In his *Diary* Sharett reports consultations with the Israeli ambassador to Brazil, David Shealtiel, concerning the settlement in that country of half a million Palestinian refugees—one hundred thousand "in the first stage." Sharett expresses enthusiasm for the project.

2. Negotiations on the implementation of a UN-approved plan for the division of Jordan River water among Israel, Syria and Jordan were conducted at the time by President Eisenhower's special envoy Eric Johnston. Israel, however, was rapidly nearing the completion of its own deviation project. No agreement was ever concluded.

3. In September 1979, following the publication of Sharett's *Diary*, an Israeli citizen on a radio debate asked Arik Sharon about the massacre, in which sixty-nine civilians were killed. Sharon, who personally commanded the Kibya action, and who was a loyal member of Mapai in the 1950s, according to Sharett, is today the minister in the Begin government responsible for the colonization of the West Bank and Gaza. A report on this radio discussion in the Histadrut-Labor Party newspaper *Davar*, of 14 September 1979, gives the following comments:

> The responsibility for the killing of 69 civilians in Kibya, according to Sharon, falls on the victims themselves. At that time the Arab population was used to the Army's reaching just the edge of the village, dynamiting just one house and leaving. Therefore, the people stayed in their houses. Thus, any attempt to claim that in Kibya there was a cold-blooded action to murder women and children should be described as a completely unfounded accusation.

> Sharon decided personally to give an energetic character to that action. He instructed that 600 kilograms of explosives be taken along. Forty-five houses in the village were marked to be blown up, among which was the school. The task force did not know that people were hiding in the cellars and the upper floors. The houses were blown up after a superficial examination of the ground floor alone. This is why the number of victims was so high.

> Kibya was, according to all evidence, a tragic error. A more cautious commander may have avoided it. Had Arik Sharon changed for the better since, he would have now said that he was sorry. He did not.

Davar editorialist Nahum Barnea ostensibly attacks Sharon, but in fact he obviously tends to excuse the murderous operation. Kibya was no "tragic error" but a deliberate crime, as the context of Sharon's story proves. Before going into action, Sharett's soldiers, moreover, were given a dramatic description of a previous incident in Yahud (an Arab village repopulated with Israeli Jews) in which a woman was killed. Yahud served as a pretext for the Kibya attack, although it was known that Kibya had no other relation to the earlier episode. Clearly, the intention was to incite the soldiers emotionally to exterminate the greatest possible number of civilians and have no qualms about the killing of women and children. Significantly, upon his return from Kibya, Sharon reported the number of victims to have been ten to twelve: "We counted only the military dead, the soldiers of the Jordanian Legion's garrison," he said in the above broadcast.

4. At that time Israel was literally flooding the world with propaganda in which it catastrophically pictured itself as threatened in its daily existence by growing Arab power. It is also significant that the above disclosures were made confidentially to American Zionist leaders, who thus became involved in Israel's two-faced strategy. The use of the term "Western Eretz Israel" is particularly illuminating. It implies that, in contrast with their official statements at that time, the concept of an "Eastern Eretz Israel" (i.e., Jordan) has never been eliminated from the political vocabulary of the Israeli leadership.

5. See *Ha'aretz* of 29 June 1979, commenting on a recent wave of terrorist actions in Syria attributed to the Muslim Brothers: "If Syria assumes its Sunni character again, as it was prior to the rise of the Ba'ath and the Alawites to power, new and varied opportunities may open up to Israel, Lebanon and the whole Middle East. In view of such a possibility Israel must keep vigilant and alert: *it must not miss an opportunity which might be unrepeatable.*" A quarter of a century later, the same formula is being used. In general, a close reading of the Israeli press through 1979 suggests that Israel is again deploying efforts in various directions to bring about the fall of Assad's regime, and to install a Damascus regime which would go along with Israeli policies. "Israel is aiming at installing a Sadat in Damascus," one Israeli political figure told us in September 1979.

6. This is not to say, obviously, that no alliance between Israel and the U.S. existed prior to 1967. Through the fifties collaboration was particularly close between Israel's special services and the CIA. It is certainly not accidental that following the Israeli leadership's outlining of plans to disrupt Lebanon, the U.S.— according to CIA director William Colby in testimony to the Senate Subcommittee on Refugees in July 1976—"supplied arms in the fifties to Christians in Lebanon in the framework of the use of religious and ethnic minorities in the fight against communism." However, starting in the summer of 1956, and going well into the sixties, Israel was dependent on France for arms supplies and could not have acted *openly* against France's wishes. The end of France's colonial war against Algeria and De Gaulle's growing impatience with Israel's arrogance led to the termination of the French-Israeli special relationship in 1967, and to its substitution by the exclusive U.S.-Israel one.

7. Israel's systematic genocide in Lebanon for over a decade, which has recently reached a degree of cynical brutality unequalled in contemporary history outside of U.S. action in Indochina, bears no justification in any case. In the light of the documentation we have presented, Israel's pretense of acting in self defense and in defense of Lebanon's Christians against PLO terror becomes even more ridiculous as well as outrageous. This pretense is all too often supported by Western media and governments. Undoubtedly, Israel's permanent representative to the UN, Yehuda Blum, counts cynically on the ignorance of the general public when he says: "Lebanon's fundamental problems date back many years. The situation in the South should be considered only a byproduct and a symptom of those problems" *(The Nation,* 15 September 1979). This is how he describes Israel's direct massacre of civilian populations and the other daily attacks, devastation and torture, carried out with U.S.-made arms and under Israeli protection by Israel's isolationist Maronite puppets commanded by Major Sa'd Haddad.

8. Sharett hinted that the report was clandestinely intercepted by the Israelis. He also aired the possibility that Hutcheson intended to refer to elements from the Irgun, acting against his government and then rejected this hypothesis. In this connection it is interesting to recall that in a debate in the Knesset *(Divrei Haknesset Hashnya,* p. 654) on January 25, 1955, a Herut spokesman, Arie Altmann, attacked the government for its "weaknesses" and added: "If the government will not comply with its duties in the security field, don't be surprised if one day you will be confronted with the surprising phenomena of private initiatives, and not one initiative, but a very complex and ramified one . . . ." In his *Mistraim Ve'Ha Fedayeen* (see note 20) Ehud Ya'ari mentions the existence at that time of a terrorist group operating in border areas under the name of "Tadmor Group" of which, he says, "no details are yet available." These disclosures suggest that a close cooperation existed at that time, on an operative-clandestine level, between the pre-state terrorist Zionist organizations—the Irgun and the Stern gang, which were officially dissolved in 1948 but in fact continued to act militarily—and regular army or "security" units such as the paratroopers corps and

Sharon's Unit 101. The latter, Ya'ari recalls, "operated its own unpublicized 'infiltrations' into the Gaza Strip...accomplishing actions such as the attack on the refugee camp at Al Burj, near Gaza, on August 31, 1953." Further research on this subject might reveal that the extent of the acts of aggressive provocations by Israeli forces across the armistice lines were much vaster than has ever been known publicly. However, the most important aspect of these relations lies in their political significance, which offers a completely new key to the interpretation of the history of the Zionist state. In fact, they constitute a decisive refutation of the accepted thesis according to which a distinct division, marked by ideological, political and pragmatic antagonisms, existed at least up to 1965 between labour Zionism and the so-called "irrational Zionism" of Revisionist origin.

9. Israel launched a particularly virulent campaign about Ma'aleh Ha'akrabim, and renewed the campaign at the time of, and as a justification of, the 1956 attack on Egypt.

10. The euphemistic use of the term "retaliation" in the context of actions to be realized according to a pre-fixed plan corresponds to Dayan's description of the "reprisal" policy. Reminiscent of notorious euphemisms from the Vietnam war ("pacification," "neutralization," "Vietnamization"), the term has been used until recently to describe Israel's massacres in Lebanon.

11. Today Sharon is minister of agriculture in Begin's government, and responsible for the colonization of the West Bank and Gaza. He was commander of the notorious "Unit 101," which engaged in actions against civilian populations across the armistice lines. In a recent radio debate (see note 3 above), Sharon was asked about this episode. "As to Meir Hartsion," Sharon said, "I want to say: it is unfortunate that there are no more men like him, with his loyalty, his love for the country, and his contribution to raise the combat level of the Israeli army. It is shameful that a man who fought, and fought for you too, you call him a 'murderer'." (*Davar*, 14 September 1979)

12. It must be noted that the term "terrorism" was not in vogue at that time. Sharett, in fact, uses the word "revenge" and "blind revenge." It is clear that he was groping for a word that would correspond exactly to today's use of "terrorism."

13. Both texts are reproduced from the Acts of the Olshan-Dori Inquiry Commission of the "Affair," annexed to the *Diary*, pages 659, 664, respectively.

14. In a letter to Ben Gurion dated March 6, 1961 Sharett confirmed: Why did I refuse then to approve the firing of Peres? Because his removal at *that period* would have been interpreted as an admission that the leadership of Israel's security establishment was responsible for the savage actions in Cairo" (p. 789). In general, very little is known outside Israel about the "Affair" and its complicated ramifications and implications which have profoundly corroded and influenced Israel's political life for years. It is therefore understandable that even an excellent reporter such as David Hirst could be misled to think that Lavon shared Sharett's moderate line (*The Gun and the Olive Branch*, London: Futura Publications, 1976). In fact Lavon was an ardent "activist" who missed no occasion to preach the use of violence and this was why Ben Gurion, when leaving for Sdeh Boker, left him in charge of "his" defense ministry. Later, however, Ben Gurion began to suspect that through his activist zeal, Lavon also sought to supplant him at the head of the security establishment. Thus, a complicated rivalry involving these two members of Mapai's leadership as well, as for their own reasons and ambitions, Ben Gurion's younger heirs, especially Peres and Dayan, became interwoven in the intrigues to which the "Affair" had given rise.

15. *Ahdut Ha'avoda*, whose best known leaders were Yigal Allon and Israel Galili, united with Mapai to form the Labor Party in the sixties.

16. The history of the attempts to organize *coups d'etat* in Israel is also little known outside its borders. In 1957 one such attempt was plotted by a group of

officers who wished to prevent the retreat from Gaza and Sinai, which Ben Gurion had reluctantly accepted under heavy international pressure. In late May 1967, it was under the threat of a military coup that Premier Levi Eshkol co-opted opposition Knesset member Moshe Dayan into his government as minister of defense, thereby definitely acquiescing in the army's decision to go to war.

17. This comment was made by Lewis Jones, an embassy aide in Cairo, who Sharett says "is considered a personal friend of Nahum Goldman and Teddy Kollek and is well known to us for his fair attitude to Israel." Jones also expressed the opinion that Israeli protests against the Cairo sentences should not be taken too seriously: "Even if there will be a hanging [death sentence] it would not be a disaster [for the Israelis]... since it will probably help [the Israelis] to collect more money in the U.S." (8 February 1955, p. 712)

18. (7 October 1955, p. 1197). See also Kenneth Love, *Suez* (McGraw-Hill, 1969). Sharett here told the story of how a previous news agency dispatch on the interview with Love, attributed to Nasser the phrase "we should destroy Israel." Sharett couldn't believe this to be true, and he professed to have been relieved when the correction of what was reported as a "telex transmission error" arrived, confirming his own view of Nasser's conciliatory policies.

19. A detailed comparison of the above realities with, among others, the account and analysis of the events of that period as provided by Nadav Safran in his *Israel— The Embattled Ally* (Cambridge: Harvard University Press, 1978) would throw a significant light on the falsifications that continue to permeate a certain Zionist-inspired historiography to this day. According to Safran, Nasser's attitude shifted in 1955 "from one of apparent moderation to one that seemed bent on... leading the Arab States in an assault on Israel" and the "apparent willingness of the Arab States to accept a Jewish State" changed in the mid-fifties to a "commitment to eliminate that State." (See also note 20.)

20. See Abu Iyad, *Palestinien Sans Patrie* (Paris: n.p., 1979) and Ehud Ya'ari, *Mitsraim Ve'Ha Fedayeen* (Givat Haviva, 1975). The first, by one of the leading figures of Fatah, provides a direct account, from personal experience, of the Egyptian repression of the attempts by the Palestinian refugees in Gaza to organize resistance cells. The second consists of a collection of documents captured by the Israeli intelligence during the 1956 and 1967 wars in Gaza, Sinai and the West Bank, which demonstrate the efforts by the Egyptian and Jordanian governments to suppress any infiltration to Israel, control the borders, and repress the demands by the population for adequate defense measures to protect them against Israeli incursions, including the demand for a distribution of arms. The following constitute the main points in the evidence contained in Ya'ari's documents:

— At the end of 1953, the Egyptian administration of Gaza reported to the War Ministry in Cairo on arrests of infiltrators and actions to block their access routes to the border. At that same time police and army troops were employed in refugee camps attacked by Israel to disperse demonstrators asking for arms and protesting plans to settle Palestinian refugees in an area near Al Arish.

— A special civil guard force was created at the end of 1953 to control the Palestinian refugee camps.

— In 1954 this force was reenforced. In that year, the Egyptian representative in the Mixed Armistice Commission replied to a complaint by Israeli representative Arie Shalev in regard to infiltrations: "We are not sending them, and as far as we are concerned, you can kill them."

— "There is not one single Egyptian document [among those captured and examined] that speaks positively of infiltrations or sabotage actions. On the contrary, they all reflect an official policy of suppression and energetic directives to this effect," according to Ya'ari's conclusion. This has been confirmed also from other sources:

General E. L. M. Burns, who was the head of the UN Observers Corps in the Middle East, reported in his book *Between Arab and Israeli* (London: n.p., 1962) that Nasser told him in November 1954 that he wanted calm to reign in the Gaza Strip.

Keith Wheelock, in his *Nasser's New Egypt* (London: n.p., 1960) wrote that ". . . it was clear that the Egyptian government wishes to avoid fighting along the border, if only because the great plan for internal development left very limited resources for a reenforcement of the Egyptian army."

Among the documents presented by Ya'ari there is also a memorandum of a meeting held at the office of the Egyptian governor of the Gaza Strip, Yussef Al Agrudi, on January 29, 1955, one month before the Israeli attack on Gaza, in which the following measures aimed at controlling the border were decided among the rest:

—Prohibition of traffic from sunset to dawn in the area east of the Gaza-Rafah road, including the refugee camp of Jebelyiah.

—An order to open fire on any infiltrator. All the mukhtars (village chiefs) were required to report persons missing from their villages or tribes. Warnings were to be issued through the media against infiltration. A detention camp was to be set up for persons suspected of infiltration against whom no sufficient evidence existed to bring them to trial.

—Distribution of food rations to refugees who did not appear personally to receive the rations would be stopped.

According to Ya'ari, finally:

> The Israeli army attack on Gaza on February 28, 1955 was . . . a decisive turning point in the relations between Israel and Egypt. Nasser as well as many Western diplomats and analysts have spoken of it as a turning point in Cairo's policies. Nasser himself explained on innumerable occasions that the attack was the moment of truth in which he understood there was no chance for the [conciliatory] line adopted by Egypt until then. He finally perceived the dimensions of the Israeli problem, and therefore appealed for Soviet armaments . . .
>
> The [Gaza] action occurred at a moment of relative tranquility following the enforcement of repressive measures decided on by the Egyptian administration in the Strip. Hence, the explanation for Ben Gurion's decision to order the attack . . . is to be sought elsewhere.

The Israeli attack on Gaza unleashed huge demonstrations in the Strip and clashes between the local population and the Egyptian army. Due to further Israeli provocations the protests continued, and in May the Egyptian government was forced to consent to the activities of fedayeen units for sabotage actions in Israel. These units were, however, placed under the strict control of the Egyptian army, so that their activity could again be limited several months later. "In any case," is Ya'ari's conclusion, "there is no doubt that the appearance of fedayeen under direct Egyptian guidance was a phenomenon which emerged following the Israeli attack on Gaza,"

It is worth mentioning here that the documents presented by Ya'ari also include detailed information on two terrorist actions undertaken by Israeli intelligence in July 1956. In both cases senior Egyptian officers were killed by explosive packages, disguised as books. In the first case, the victim was Lt. General Mustafa Hafez, the commander of Egyptian intelligence in the Gaza Strip. Hafez emerges from the documents as a man who opposed infiltrations into Israel as well as the inclusion of Palestinians in the Civil Guard. In fact in a forged version of the circumstances of his assassination, Israel tried to attribute the murder to a settling of accounts on behalf of outraged refugees, having obviously reason to believe that this version would be accepted as credible. The other victim was the Egyptian military attache in Amman who was, according to Ya'ari, Hafez's collaborator in the recruitment of fedayeen and their infiltration into Israel from Jordanian territory. Ya'ari states that on the basis of the documents in his possession, the contradiction in the description of Hafez's role remains unsolved. The episodes, however, conform to Sharett's conviction in regard to the unrestrained use of terrorism by Israel's security establishment.

On the other hand, Sharett's *Diary* confirms beyond any doubt that Israel's security establishment strongly opposed all border security arrangements proposed by Egypt, Jordan or the UN.

A UN-Egyptian proposal that mixed Egyptian-Israeli-UN patrols operate along the borders to prevent infiltration and mining came to Dayan's knowledge, Sharett noted. The chief of staff exploded with rage. "But I don't want the UN to prevent mining!" Obviously, he considered the deterrent effect of the mixed patrols proposal on Israeli incursions *into* the Strip (see note 8) as more damaging to Israel's security than the occasional infiltrations *from* the Strip into Israel. In fact, Ben Gurion also rejected the proposal on the grounds that it "will tie our hands."

21. See Noam Chomsky in *The Nation*, 22–29 July 1978, pp. 83–88 for a review of five books on U.S.-Israeli relations, and his article "Civilized Terrorism" in *Seven Days*, July 1976, pp. 22–23.

The Association of Arab-American University Graduates, Inc. (AAUG), founded in 1967, is a non-profit, tax-exempt, educational and cultural organization dedicated to fostering better understanding between the Arab and American peoples, and promoting informed discussion of critical issues concerning the Arab world and the United States. In addition to publishing books, papers and periodicals on Arab and Arab-American affairs, the Arab-Israeli conflict, and U.S. foreign policy, the AAUG organizes conferences, seminars, and an annual convention; sponsors delegations to the Middle East; provides speakers for public forums; supports human rights and civil liberties; and helps bring its members' professional skills to bear on socio-economic needs in the Arab world.

For more information, write:

AAUG
556 Trapelo Road
Belmont, MA 02178